ISBN 978-1-330-19289-4
PIBN 10049230

1 MONTH OF
FREE
READING

at
www.ForgottenBooks.com

By purchasing this book you are eligible for one month membership to ForgottenBooks.com, giving you unlimited access to our entire collection of over 1,000,000 titles via our web site and mobile apps.

To claim your free month visit:
www.forgottenbooks.com/free49230

English
Français
Deutsche
Italiano
Español
Português

www.forgottenbooks.com

Mythology Photography **Fiction**
Fishing Christianity **Art** Cooking
Essays Buddhism Freemasonry
Medicine **Biology** Music **Ancient
Egypt** Evolution Carpentry Physics
Dance Geology **Mathematics** Fitness
Shakespeare **Folklore** Yoga Marketing
Confidence Immortality Biographies
Poetry **Psychology** Witchcraft
Electronics Chemistry History **Law**
Accounting **Philosophy** Anthropology
Alchemy Drama Quantum Mechanics
Atheism Sexual Health **Ancient History**
Entrepreneurship Languages Sport
Paleontology Needlework Islam
Metaphysics Investment Archaeology
Parenting Statistics Criminology
Motivational

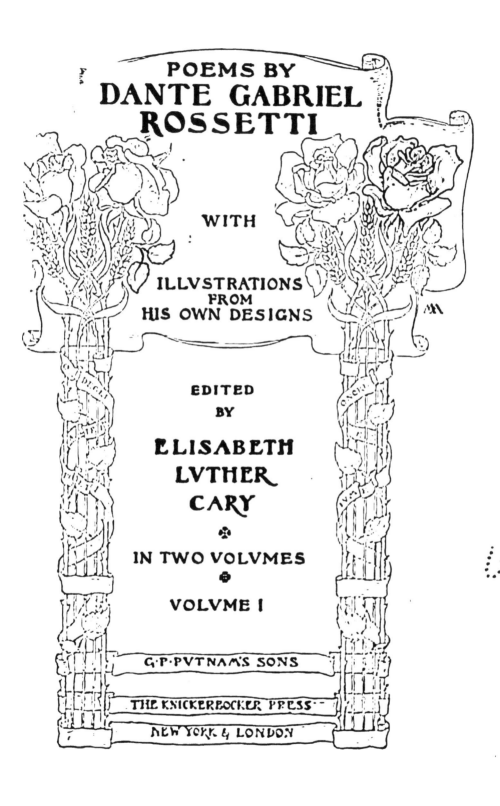

POEMS BY
DANTE GABRIEL
ROSSETTI

WITH

ILLVSTRATIONS
FROM
HIS OWN DESIGNS

EDITED
BY

ELISABETH
LVTHER
CARY

IN TWO VOLVMES

VOLVME I

G·P·PVTNAM'S SONS

THE KNICKERBOCKER PRESS

NEW YORK & LONDON

The Knickerbocker Press, New York

EDITOR'S PREFACE

THAT Rossetti's poems should be accompanied by illustrations from his own drawings is so obviously appropriate as to call for little explanation. With Rossetti painting and poetry marched together through long periods, and while he was, perhaps, more painter than poet, he was a poet before he was a painter. At the age of five he had formed the habit, never entirely relinquished, of copying his original verse into a note-book. His first long poem, a ballad called *Sir Hugh the Heron,* was written in 1841 when he was thirteen. Three years later he made a very creditable translation of Bürger's *Lenore,* and followed this with translations of two other German poems. By the time he was seventeen he had begun to translate the early Italian poets with the combined truth and felicity possible only to a mind both scholarly and poetic. Before he was nineteen he had written *The Blessed Damozel,* embodying the profound mysticism of his temperament in verse as limpid and passionate as any achieved by him in later life. All this before he had touched brush to palette for serious accomplishment, although he began to study drawing when he was about fifteen.

That he finally chose painting as a practical vocation was due to his faith in its usefulness as a means of livelihood rather than to his belief in its superiority as a method of self-expression. While he was struggling with the technical problems of the two arts, and finding poetry in those early years by far the easier of the two, he ardently considered the possibility of giving up his time to it, and wrote to Leigh Hunt for advice. The older and more sadly experienced poet replied that poetry "is not a thing for a man to live upon while he is in the flesh, however immortal it may render him in spirit." The Rossetti family were not in a position to ignore material returns, and poetry became a subordinate feature in Dante Gabriel's career.

He continued, however, to write more or less from time to time, and during the last two or three years of his life his interest in his poems was intense.

Both his poetry and his painting reveal the same side of his nature, but his brooding mind, his symbolic tendency, his egoistic vision, his exotic taste, are shown in his pictures more definitely and impressively than in his poems, where involved constructions and occasionally tortured metaphors also obscure to a degree the beauty of his poetic imagination. Highly as he valued the invisible and spiritual, and fervently as he strove to represent them through such symbols as earth and the earthly provide, it was his ironical fate to dwell so insistently upon the physical world as to give through the greater part of his poems the impression of almost complete preoccupation with it. In his paintings we find large arms and full lips and unnatural necks, but we find also haunting, spiritual eyes whose outlook is beyond the bounds of temporal life, lending an element of grave and mystical charm to the conception. And we find beside, colour so deep, so splendid, and so sombre as to enforce the impression of beauty against all interruptions by accidental detail. In his poetry we are more conscious of the limitations and defects of his taste. The sounds and rhythms, treated in a manner quite un-English and remarkable for sonorous weight and superbly balanced measure, are in many instances altogether insufficient to cover the essential poverty of the thought, and we continually miss the note of spontaneity, of inspiration, and inevitableness. Thus, frequently in the case of a painting and a poem on the same subject, Rossetti's meaning is more adequately and convincingly expressed in the former than in the latter. Occasionally, however, precisely the opposite is true. If we consider, for example, such a picture as his *Fiammetta,* and the sonnet written to accompany it, we see readily enough how the revelation of his meaning is aided by the union of the two arts. In the picture he has placed the figure of a beautiful girl among branches of apple-blossoms. She holds a spray high above her and a bird is seen perching on it. A nimbus of light surrounds her head and her eyes look out from the canvas with a direct and pensive gaze. There is plentiful suggestion in the strong figure with its surrounding flood of Spring bloom, but it would not in itself interpret the particular thought in Rossetti's mind which finds expression in the sonnet, the exquisite definition adding to the *Fiammetta* a spiritual grace for the least sympathetic beholder.

To feel to the full the passionate romanticism of Rossetti's Italian and mediæval temper, and to appreciate the noble flashes of moral insight by which his mental attitude is illumined, it is necessary to study his poems and pictures side by side, an opportunity for which this little collection offers a very pitiful substitute. And more is needed than even close familiarity with Rossetti's work to discover the side of his remarkable personality that so much endeared him to his friends. Nothing that he has painted or written for the general public suggests that frank, infectious laughter, that incisive speech akin to wit, that ready generosity of mood by which he was known within his circle. Like the great Florentine whose name he bears, the gaiety of his manner and the boyishness of his speech were curiously at variance with the deep and sober sentiment of his accomplishment. In quoting from his letters and comments on his own work I have to a slight degree suggested this free and hearty openness which was characteristic of him from his youth to the years of his decline. In this way I have tried to furnish the reader with a more satisfactory mental picture of him than could otherwise be obtained within such narrow limits.

I have not attempted exhaustive annotation. The variations in different editions of the poems I have noted when they seemed to me worthy of consideration, and many of my biographical notes have been made purely with the idea of connecting the work with the man in a way to add to the reader's interest in both.

I have arranged the poems as nearly as possible in chronological order, believing that to be the only way to gain a connected idea of the growth of a writer's mind and the continuity of his ideal. The arrangement of the *House of Life* I have not disturbed, but I have indicated the dates of the different sonnets whenever I could determine them. No one knows better than myself how little this edition of Rossetti's poems can lay claim to the honourable epithet " scholarly," but I have tried to make it the kind of edition that seems to be most valuable for a student's purposes. I have tried, that is, to arouse curiosity concerning the complex and interesting temperament of which the poems and pictures together are but an imperfect manifestation.

E. L. C.

CONTENTS

Contents

Contents

ILLUSTRATIONS.

Illustrations.

POEMS BY
DANTE GABRIEL ROSSETTI

THE BRIDE'S PRELUDE.

THE poem now called *The Bride's Prelude* was begun about 1847, and was then called *Bride-Chamber Talk*. Rossetti's own verdict on it was: "I think the poem is saved by its picturesqueness, but that otherwise the story up to the point reached is too purely repellent." He had in mind a sequel in which a nobler love should follow "the mere passionate frailty" of the first, this later love being rendered calamitous by the return of the false first lover, now desirous to marry the lady, whose brothers urge on the suit. The second lover is treacherously slain by the first in a tournament; and the marriage is agreed upon. The poem was to close with the bridal procession and an intimation of the brothers' intention to kill the bridegroom after the ceremony, they having no love for him, but viewing his alliance with their sister as a matter of expediency. "The poem would gain so greatly by this sequel," Rossetti wrote to Hall Caine, "that I suppose I must set to and finish it one day, old as it is." But this he never did. In the same letter he called the card-playing passage "the best thing — as a unit — in the poem," and explained the slow movement which was against the rule he usually followed by the fact that in place of a "life condensed in an episode," he had here "a story which had necessarily to be told step by step, and a situation which had unavoidably to be anatomised."

THE BRIDE'S PRELUDE.

(Begun in 1847.   Unfinished.)

" SISTER," said busy Amelotte
    To listless Aloÿse;
" Along your wedding-road the wheat
Bends as to hear your horse's feet,
And the noonday stands still for heat."

Amelotte laughed into the air
    With eyes that sought the sun:
But where the walls in long brocade
Were screened, as one who is afraid
Sat Aloÿse within the shade.

And even in shade was gleam enough
    To shut out full repose
From the bride's 'tiring-chamber, which
Was like the inner altar-niche
Whose dimness worship has made rich.

Within the window's heaped recess
    The light was counterchanged
In blent reflexes manifold
From perfume-caskets of wrought gold
And gems the bride's hair could not hold

All thrust together: and with these
    A slim-curved lute, which now,

The Bride's Prelude.

At Amelotte's sudden passing there,
Was swept in somewise unaware,
And shook to music the close air.

Against the haloed lattice-panes
    The bridesmaid sunned her breast;
Then to the glass turned tall and free,
And braced and shifted daintily
Her loin-belt through her côte-hardie.

The belt was silver, and the clasp
    Of lozenged arm-bearings;
A world of mirrored tints minute
The rippling sunshine wrought into 't,
That flushed her hand and warmed her foot.

At least an hour had Aloÿse,—
    Her jewels in her hair,—
Her white gown, as became a bride,
Quartered in silver at each side,—
Sat thus aloof, as if to hide.

Over her bosom, that lay still,
    The vest was rich in grain,
With close pearls wholly overset:
Around her throat the fastenings met
Of chevesayle and mantelet.

Her arms were laid along her lap
    With the hands open: life
Itself did seem at fault in her:
Beneath the drooping brows, the stir
Of thought made noonday heavier.

The Bride's Prelude.

Long sat she silent; and then raised
　　Her head, with such a gasp
As while she summoned breath to speak
Fanned high that furnace in the cheek
But sucked the heart-pulse cold and weak.

(Oh gather round her now, all ye
　　Past seasons of her fear,—
Sick springs, and summers deadly cold!
To flight your hovering wings unfold,
For now your secret shall be told.

Ye many sunlights, barbed with darts
　　Of dread detecting flame,—
Gaunt moonlights that like sentinels
Went past with iron clank of bells,—
Draw round and render up your spells!)

"Sister," said Aloÿse, "I had
　　A thing to tell thee of
Long since, and could not.　But do thou
Kneel first in prayer awhile, and bow
Thine heart, and I will tell thee now."

Amelotte wondered with her eyes;
　　But her heart said in her:
"Dear Aloÿse would have me pray
Because the awe she feels to-day
Must need more prayers than she can say."

So Amelotte put by the folds
　　That covered up her feet,
And knelt,— beyond the arras'd gloom
And the hot window's dull perfume,—
Where day was stillest in the room.

The Bride's Prelude.

"Queen Mary, hear," she said, "and say
    To Jesus the Lord Christ,
This bride's new joy, which He confers,
New joy to many ministers,
And many griefs are bound in hers."

The bride turned in her chair, and hid
    Her face against the back,
And took her pearl-girt elbows in
Her hands, and could not yet begin,
But shuddering, uttered, "Urscelyn!"

Most weak she was; for as she pressed
    Her hand against her throat,
Along the arras she let trail
Her face, as if all heart did fail,
And sat with shut eyes, dumb and pale.

Amelotte still was on her knees
    As she had kneeled to pray.
Deeming her sister swooned, she thought,
At first, some succour to have brought;
But Aloÿse rocked, as one distraught.

She would have pushed the lattice wide
    To gain what breeze might be;
But marking that no leaf once beat
The outside casement, it seemed meet
Not to bring in more scent and heat.

So she said only: "Aloÿse,
    Sister, when happened it
At any time that the bride came
To ill, or spoke in fear of shame
When speaking first the bridegroom's name?"

The Bride's Prelude.

A bird had out its song and ceased
    Ere the bride spoke.   At length
She said: " The name is as the thing:—
Sin hath no second christening,
And shame is all that shame can bring.

" In divers places many an while
    I would have told thee this;
But faintness took me, or a fit
Like fever.   God would not permit
That I should change thine eyes with it.

" Yet once I spoke, hadst thou but heard: —
    That time we wandered out
All the sun's hours, but missed our way
When evening darkened, and so lay
The whole night covered up in hay.

" At last my face was hidden: so,
    Having God's hint, I paused
Not long; but drew myself more near
Where thou wast laid, and shook off fear,
And whispered quick into thine ear

" Something of the whole tale.   At first
    I lay and bit my hair
For the sore silence thou didst keep:
Till, as thy breath came long and deep,
I knew that thou hadst been asleep.

" The moon was covered, but the stars
    Lasted till morning broke.
Awake, thou told'st me that thy dream
Had been of me,— that all did seem
At jar,— but that it was a dream.

The Bride's Prelude.

"I knew God's hand and might not speak.
    After that night I kept
Silence and let the record swell:
Till now there is much more to tell
Which must be told out ill or well."

She paused then, weary, with dry lips
    Apart.   From the outside
By fits there boomed a dull report
From where i' the hanging tennis-court
The bridegroom's retinue made sport.

The room lay still in dusty glare,
    Having no sound through it
Except the chirp of a caged bird
That came and ceased: and if she stirred,
Amelotte's raiment could be heard. ·

Quoth Amelotte: " The night this chanced
    Was a late summer night
Last year! What secret, for Christ's love,
Keep'st thou since then ? Mary above!
What thing is this thou speakest of ?

"Mary and Christ! Lest when 't is told
    I should be prone to wrath,—
This prayer beforehand! How she errs
Soe'er, take count of grief like hers,
Whereof the days are turned to years! "

She bowed her neck, and having said,
    Kept on her knees to hear;
And then, because strained thought demands
Quiet before it understands,
Darkened her eyesight with her hands.

The Bride's Prelude.

So when at last her sister spoke,
    She did not see the pain
O' the mouth nor the ashamèd eyes,
But marked the breath that came in sighs
And the half-pausing for replies.

This was the bride's sad prelude-strain:—
    "I' the convent where a girl
I dwelt till near my womanhood,
I had but preachings of the rood
And Aves told in solitude

"To spend my heart on: and my hand
    Had but the weary skill
To eke out upon silken cloth
Christ's visage, or the long bright growth
Of Mary's hair, or Satan wroth.

"So when at last I went, and thou,
    A child not known before,
Didst come to take the place I left,—
My limbs, after such lifelong theft
Of life, could be but little deft

" In all that ministers delight
    To noble women: I
Had learned no word of youth's discourse,
Nor gazed on games of warriors,
Nor trained a hound, nor ruled a horse.

"Besides, the daily life i' the sun
    Made me at first hold back.
To thee this came at once; to me
It crept with pauses timidly;
I am not blithe and strong like thee.

The Bride's Prelude.

" Yet my feet like the dances well,
    The songs went to my voice,
The music made me shake and weep;
And often, all night long, my sleep
Gave dreams I had been fain to keep.

" But though I loved not holy things,
    To hear them scorned brought pain,—
They were my childhood; and these dames
Were merely perjured in saints' names
And fixed upon saints' days for games.

"And sometimes when my father rode
    To hunt with his loud friends,
I dared not bring him to be quaff'd,
As my wont was, his stirrup-draught,
Because they jested so and laugh'd.

" At last one day my brothers said,
    ' The girl must not grow thus,—
Bring her a jennet,—she shall ride.'
They helped my mounting, and I tried
To laugh with them and keep their side.

" But brakes were rough and bents were steep
    Upon our path that day:
My palfrey threw me; and I went
Upon men's shoulders home, sore spent,
While the chase followed up the scent.

"Our shrift-father (and he alone
    Of all the household there
Had skill in leechcraft,) was away
When I reached home. I tossed, and lay
Sullen with anguish the whole day.

The Bride's Prelude.

"For the day passed ere some one brought
    To mind that in the hunt
Rode a young lord she named, long bred
Among the priests, whose art (she said)
Might chance to stand me in much stead.

"I bade them seek and summon him:
    But long ere this, the chase
Had scattered, and he was not found.
I lay in the same weary stound,
Therefore, until the night came round.

"It was dead night and near on twelve
    When the horse-tramp at length
Beat up the echoes of the court:
By then, my feverish breath was short
With pain the sense could scarce support.

"My fond nurse sitting near my feet
    Rose softly,—her lamp's flame
Held in her hand, lest it should make
My heated lids, in passing, ache;
And she passed softly, for my sake.

"Returning soon, she brought the youth
    They spoke of.   Meek he seemed,
But good knights held him of stout heart.
He was akin to us in part,
And bore our shield, but barred athwart.

"I now remembered to have seen
    His face, and heard him praised
For letter-lore and medicine,
Seeing his youth was nurtured in
Priests' knowledge, as mine own had been."

The Bride's Prelude.

The bride's voice did not weaken here,
    Yet by her sudden pause
She seemed to look for questioning;
Or else (small need though) 't was to bring
Well to her mind the bygone thing.

Her thought, long stagnant, stirred by speech,
    Gave her a sick recoil;
As, dip thy fingers through the green
That masks a pool, — where they have been
The naked depth is black between.

Amelotte kept her knees; her face
    Was shut within her hands,
As it had been throughout the tale;
Her forehead's whiteness might avail
Nothing to say if she were pale.

Although the lattice had dropped loose,
    There was no wind; the heat
Being so at rest that Amelotte
Heard far beneath the plunge and float
Of a hound swimming in the moat.

Some minutes since, two rooks had toiled
    Home to the nests that crowned
Ancestral ash-trees.   Through the glare
Beating again, they seemed to tear
With that thick caw the woof o' the air.

But else, 't was at the dead of noon
    Absolute silence; all,
From the raised bridge and guarded sconce
To green-clad places of pleasaunce
Where the long lake was white with swans.

The Bride's Prelude.

"He made me sit. 'Cousin, I grieve
    Your sickness stays by you.'
'I would,' said I, 'that you did err
So grieving. I am wearier
Than death, of the sickening dying year.'

"He answered: If your weariness
    Accepts a remedy,
I hold one and can give it you.'
I gazed: 'What ministers thereto,
Be sure,' I said, 'that I will do.'

"He went on quickly:—'T was a cure
    He had not ever named
Unto our kin lest they should stint
Their favour, for some foolish hint
Of wizardry or magic in 't:

"But that if he were let to come
    Within my bower that night,
(My women still attending me,
He said, while he remain'd there,) he
Could teach me the cure privily.

"I bade him come that night. He came;
    But little in his speech
Was cure or sickness spoken of,
Only a passionate fierce love
That clamoured upon God above.

"My women wondered, leaning close
    Aloof. At mine own heart
I think great wonder was not stirr'd.
I dared not listen, yet I heard
His tangled speech, word within word.

Study for the lovers in the background of
" *The Blessed Damozel.*"

Version of 1876

The Bride's Prelude.

" He craved my pardon first,—all else
    Wild tumult.   In the end
He remained silent at my feet
Fumbling the rushes.   Strange quick heat
Made all the blood of my life meet.

" And lo! I loved him.   I but said,
    If he would leave me then,
His hope some future might forecast.
His hot lips stung my hand: at last
My damsels led him forth in haste."

The bride took breath to pause; and turned
    Her gaze where Amelotte
Knelt,—the gold hair upon her back
Quite still in all its threads,—the track
Of her still shadow sharp and black.

That listening without sight had grown
    To stealthy dread; and now
That the one sound she had to mark
Left her alone too, she was stark
Afraid, as children in the dark.

Her fingers felt her temples beat;
    Then came that brain-sickness
Which thinks to scream, and murmureth;
And pent between her hands, the breath
Was damp against her face like death.

Her arms both fell at once; but when
    She gasped upon the light,
Her sense returned.   She would have pray'd
To change whatever words still stay'd
Behind, but felt there was no aid.

The Bride's Prelude.

So she rose up, and having gone
    Within the window's arch
Once more, she sat there, all intent
On torturing doubts, and once more bent
To hear, in mute bewilderment.

But Aloÿse still paused.   Thereon
    Amelotte gathered voice
In somewise from the torpid fear
Coiled round her spirit.   Low but clear
She said: "Speak, sister; for I hear."

But Aloÿse threw up her neck
    And called the name of God:—
"Judge, God, 'twixt her and me to-day!
She knows how hard this is to say,
Yet will not have one word away."

Her sister was quite silent.   Then
    Afresh:—"Not she, dear Lord!
Thou be my judge. on Thee I call!"
She ceased,—her forehead smote the wall:
"Is there a God," she said, "at all?"

Amelotte shuddered at the soul,
    But did not speak.   The pause
Was long this time.   At length the bride
Pressed her hand hard against her side,
And trembling between shame and pride

Said by fierce effort: "From that night
    Often at nights we met:
That night, his passion could but rave:
The next, what grace his lips did crave
I knew not, but I know I gave."

The Bride's Prelude.

Where Amelotte was sitting, all
    The light and warmth of day
Were so upon her without shade
That the thing seemed by sunshine made
Most foul and wanton to be said.

She would have questioned more, and known
    The whole truth at its worst,
But held her silent, in mere shame
Of day.   'T was only these words came :—
" Sister, thou hast not said his name."

" Sister," quoth Aloÿse, " thou know'st
    His name.   I said that he
Was in a manner of our kin.
Waiting the title he might win,
They called him the Lord Urscelyn."

The bridgroom's name, to Amelotte
    Daily familiar,— heard
Thus in this dreadful history,—
Was dreadful to her; as might be
Thine own voice speaking unto thee.

The day's mid-hour was almost full;
    Upon the dial-plate
The angel's sword stood near at One.
An hour 's remaining yet; the sun
Will not decrease till all be done.

Through the bride's lattice there crept in
    At whiles (from where the train
Of minstrels, till the marriage-call,
Loitered at windows of the wall,)
Stray lute-notes, sweet and musical.

The Bride's Prelude.

They clung in the green growths and moss
    Against the outside stone;
Low like dirge-wail or requiem
They murmured, lost 'twixt leaf and stem:
There was no wind to carry them.

Amelotte gathered herself back
    Into the wide recess
That the sun flooded: it o'erspread
Like flame the hair upon her head
And fringed her face with burning red.

All things seemed shaken and at change:
    A silent place o' the hills
She knew, into her spirit came:
Within herself she said its name
And wondered was it still the same.

The bride (whom silence goaded) now
    Said strongly,—her despair
By stubborn will kept underneath:—
"Sister, 't were well thou didst not breathe
That curse of thine.   Give me my wreath."

"Sister," said Amelotte, "abide
    In peace.   Be God thy judge,
As thou hast said—not I.   For me,
I merely will thank God that he
Whom thou hast lovèd loveth thee."

Then Aloÿse lay back, and laughed
    With wan lips bitterly,
Saying, "Nay, thank thou God for this,—
That never any soul like his
Shall have its portion where love is."

The Bride's Prelude.

Weary of wonder, Amelotte
   Sat silent: she would ask
No more, though all was unexplained: .
She was too weak; the ache still pained
Her eyes,—her forehead's pulse remained.

The silence lengthened.   Aloÿse
   Was fain to turn her face
Apart, to where the arras told
Two Testaments, the New and Old,
In shapes and meanings manifold.

One solace that was gained, she hid.
   Her sister, from whose curse
Her heart recoiled, had blessed instead!
Yet would not her pride have it said
How much the blessing comforted.

Only, on looking round again
   After some while, the face
Which from the arras turned away
Was more at peace and less at bay
With shame than it had been that day.

She spoke right on, as if no pause
   Had come between her speech:
"That year from warmth grew bleak and pass'd,"
She said; "the days from first to last
How slow,—woe 's me! the nights how fast!

"From first to last it was not known:
   My nurse, and of my train
Some four or five, alone could tell
What terror kept inscrutable:
There was good need to guard it well.

The Bride's Prelude.

"Not the guilt only made the shame,
    But he was without land
And born amiss. He had but come
To train his youth here at our home,
And, being man, depart therefrom.

"Of the whole time each single day
    Brought fear and great unrest:
It seemed that all would not avail
Some once,—that my close watch would fail,
And some sign, somehow, tell the tale.

"The noble maidens that I knew,
    My fellows, oftentimes
Midway in talk or sport, would look
A wonder which my fears mistook,
To see how I turned faint and shook.

"They had a game of cards, where each
    By painted arms might find
What knight she should be given to,
Ever with trembling hand I threw
Lest I should learn the thing I knew.

"And once it came. And Aure d'Honvaulx
    Held up the bended shield
And laughed: 'Gramercy for our share!—
If to our bridal we but fare
To smutch the blazon that we bear!'

"But proud Denise de Villenbois
    Kissed me, and gave her wench
The card, and said: 'If in these bowers
You women play at paramours,
You must not mix your game with ours.'

The Bride's Prelude.

"And one upcast it from her hand:
　　'Lo! see how high he 'll soar!'
But then their laugh was bitterest;
For the wind veered at fate's behest
And blew it back into my breast.

"Oh! if I met him in the day
　　Or heard his voice,—at meals
Or at the Mass or through the hall,—
A look turned towards me would appal
My heart by seeming to know all.

"Yet I grew curious of my shame,
　　And sometimes in the church,
On hearing such a sin rebuked,
Have held my girdle-glass unhooked
To see how such a woman looked.

"But if at night he did not come,
　　I lay all deadly cold
To think they might have smitten sore
And slain him, and as the night wore,
His corpse be lying at my door.

"And entering or going forth,
　　Our proud shield o'er the gate
Seemed to arraign my shrinking eyes.
With tremors and unspoken lies
The year went past me in this wise.

"About the spring of the next year
　　An ailing fell on me;
(I had been stronger till the spring;)
'T was mine old sickness gathering,
I thought; but 't was another thing.

[23]

The Bride's Prelude.

"I had such yearnings as brought tears,
        And a wan dizziness:
Motion, like feeling, grew intense;
Sight was a haunting evidence
And sound a pang that snatched the sense.

"It now was hard on that great ill
        Which lost our wealth from us
And all our lands.   Accursed be
The peevish fools of liberty
Who will not let themselves be free!

"The Prince was fled into the west:
        A price was on his blood,
But he was safe.   To us his friends
He left that ruin which attends
The strife against God's secret ends.

"The league dropped all asunder,— lord,
        Gentle and serf.   Our house
Was marked to fall.   And a day came
When half the wealth that propped our name
Went from us in a wind of flame.

"Six hours I lay upon the wall
        And saw it burn.   But when
It clogged the day in a black bed
Of louring vapour, I was led
Down to the postern, and we fled.

"But ere we fled, there was a voice
        Which I heard speak, and say
That many of our friends, to shun
Our fate, had left us and were gone,
And that Lord Urscelyn was one.

The Bride's Prelude.

"That name, as was its wont, made sight
    And hearing whirl. I gave
No heed but only to the name:
I held my senses, dreading them,
And was at strife to look the same.

"We rode and rode. As the speed grew,
    The growth of some vague curse
Swarmed in my brain. It seemed to me
Numbed by the swiftness, but would be —
That still — clear knowledge certainly.

"Night lapsed. At dawn the sea was there
    And the sea-wind: afar
The ravening surge was hoarse and loud
And underneath the dim dawn-cloud
Each stalking wave shook like a shroud.

"From my drawn litter I looked out
    Unto the swarthy sea,
And knew. That voice, which late had cross'd
Mine ears, seemed with the foam uptoss'd:
I knew that Urscelyn was lost.

"Then I spake all: I turned on one
    And on the other, and spake:
My curse laughed in me to behold
Their eyes: I sat up, stricken cold,
Mad of my voice till all was told.

"Oh! of my brothers, Hugues was mute,
    And Gilles was wild and loud,
And Raoul strained abroad his face,
As if his gnashing wrath could trace
Even there the prey that it must chase.

The Bride's Prelude.

"And round me murmured all our train,
　　Hoarse as the hoarse-tongued sea;
Till Hugues from silence louring woke,
And cried: 'What ails the foolish folk?
Know ye not frenzy's lightning-stroke?'

"But my stern father came to them
　　And quelled them with his look,
Silent and deadly pale.　Anon
I knew that we were hastening on,
My litter closed and the light gone.

"And I remember all that day
　　 The barren bitter wind
Without, and the sea's moaning there
That I first moaned with unaware,
And when I knew, shook down my hair.

"Few followed us or faced our flight:
　　Once only I could hear,
Far in the front, loud scornful words,
And cries I knew of hostile lords,
And crash of spears and grind of swords.

"It was soon ended.　On that day
　　Before the light had changed
We reached our refuge; miles of rock
Bulwarked for war; whose strength might mock
Sky, sea, or man, to storm or shock.

"Listless and feebly conscious, I
　　Lay far within the night
Awake.　The many pains incurred
That day,—the whole, said, seen or heard,—
Stayed by in me as things deferred.

The Bride's Prelude.

"Not long. At dawn I slept. In dreams
    All was passed through afresh
From end to end. As the morn heaved
Towards noon, I, waking sore aggrieved,
That I might die, cursed God, and lived.

"Many days went, and I saw none
    Except my women. They
Calmed their wan faces, loving me;
And when they wept, lest I should see,
Would chaunt a desolate melody.

"Panic unthreatened shook my blood
    Each sunset, all the slow
Subsiding of the turbid light.
I would rise, sister, as I might,
And bathe my forehead through the night

"To elude madness. The stark walls
    Made chill the mirk: and when
We oped our curtains, to resume
Sun-sickness after long sick gloom,
The withering sea-wind walked the room.

"Through the gaunt windows the great gales
    Bore in the tattered clumps
Of waif-weed and the tamarisk-boughs;
And sea-mews, 'mid the storm's carouse,
Were flung, wild-clamouring, in the house.

"My hounds I had not; and my hawk,
    Which they had saved for me,
Wanting the sun and rain to beat
His wings, soon lay with gathered feet;
And my flowers faded, lacking heat.

The Bride's Prelude.

"Such still were griefs: for grief was still
    A separate sense, untouched
Of that despair which had become
My life. Great anguish could benumb
My soul,—my heart was quarrelsome.

"Time crept. Upon a day at length
    My kinsfolk sat with me:
That which they asked was bare and plain:
I answered: the whole bitter strain
Was again said, and heard again.

"Fierce Raoul snatched his sword, and turned
    The point against my breast.
I bared it, smiling: 'To the heart
Strike home,' I said; 'another dart
Wreaks hourly there a deadlier smart.'

"'Twas then my sire struck down the sword,
    And said with shaken lips:
'She from whom all of you receive
Your life, so smiled; and I forgive.'
Thus, for my mother's sake, I live.

"But I, a mother even as she,
    Turned shuddering to the wall:
For I said: 'Great God! and what would I do,
When to the sword, with the thing I knew,
I offered not one life but two!'

"Then I fell back from them, and lay
    Outwearied. My tired sense
Soon filmed and settled, and like stone
I slept; till something made me moan,
And I woke up at night alone.

The Bride's Prelude.

"I woke at midnight, cold and dazed;
    Because I found myself
Seated upright, with bosom bare,
Upon my bed, combing my hair,
Ready to go, I knew not where.

"It dawned light day,—the last of those
    Long months of longing days.
That noon, the change was wrought on me
In somewise,—nought to hear or see,—
Only a trance and agony."

The bride's voice failed her, from no will
    To pause.   The bridesmaid leaned,
And where the window-panes were white,
Looked for the day: she knew not quite
If there were either day or night.

It seemed to Aloÿse that the whole
    Day's weight lay back on her
Like lead.   The hours that did remain
Beat their dry wings upon her brain
Once in mid-flight, and passed again.

There hung a cage of burnt perfumes
    In the recess: but these,
For some hours, weak against the sun,
Had simmered in white ash.   From One
The second quarter was begun.

They had not heard the stroke.   The air,
    Though altered with no wind,
Breathed now by pauses, so to say:
Each breath was time that went away,—
Each pause a minute of the day.

The Bride's Prelude.

I' the almonry, the almoner,
    Hard by, had just dispensed
Church-dole and march-dole. High and wide
Now rose the shout of thanks, which cried
On God that He should bless the bride.

Its echo thrilled within their feet,
    And in the furthest rooms
Was heard, where maidens flushed and gay
Wove with stooped necks the wreaths alway
Fair for the virgin's marriage-day.

The mother leaned along, in thought
    After her child; till tears,
Bitter, not like a wedded girl's,
Fell down her breast along her curls,
And ran in the close work of pearls.

The speech ached at her heart. She said:
    "Sweet Mary, do thou plead
This hour with thy most blessed Son
To let these shameful words atone,
That I may die when I have done."

The thought ached at her soul. Yet now:—
    "Itself—that life" (she said,)
"Out of my weary life—when sense
Unclosed, was gone. What evil men's
Most evil hands had borne it thence

"I knew, and cursed them. Still in sleep
    I have my child; and pray
To know if it indeed appear
As in my dream's perpetual sphere,
That I—death reached—may seek it there.

The Bride's Prelude.

"Sleeping, I wept; though until dark
    A fever dried mine eyes
Kept open; save when a tear might
Be forced from the mere ache of sight.
And I nursed hatred day and night.

"Aye, and I sought revenge by spells;
    And vainly many a time
Have laid my face into the lap
Of a wise woman, and heard clap
Her thunder, the fiend's juggling trap.

"At length I feared to curse them, lest
    From evil lips the curse
Should be a blessing; and would sit
Rocking myself and stifling it
With babbled jargon of no wit.

"But this was not at first: the days
    And weeks made frenzied months
Before this came. My curses, pil'd
Then with each hour unreconcil'd,
Still wait for those who took my child."

She stopped, grown fainter. "Amelotte,
    Surely," she said, "this sun
Sheds judgment-fire from the fierce south:
It does not let me breathe: the drouth
Is like sand spread within my mouth."

The bridesmaid rose. I' the outer glare
    Gleamed her pale cheeks, and eyes
Sore troubled; and aweary weigh'd
Her brows just lifted out of shade;
And the light jarred within her head.

[31]

The Bride's Prelude.

'Mid flowers fair-heaped there stood a bowl
    With water.   She therein
Through eddying bubbles slid a cup,
And offered it, being risen up,
Close to her sister's mouth, to sup.

The freshness dwelt upon her sense, .
    Yet did not the bride drink;
But she dipped in her hand anon
And cooled her temples; and all wan
With lids that held their ache, went on.

"Through those dark watches of my woe,
    Time, an ill plant, had waxed
Apace.   That year was finished.   Dumb
And blind, life's wheel with earth's had come
Whirled round: and we might seek our home.

"Our wealth was rendered back, with wealth
    Snatched from our foes.   The house
Had more than its old strength and fame:
But still 'neath the fair outward claim
I rankled,—a fierce core of shame.

"It chilled me from their eyes and lips
    Upon a night of those
First days of triumph, as I gazed
Listless and sick, or scarcely raised
My face to mark the sports they praised.

" The endless changes of the dance
    Bewildered me: the tones
Of lute and cithern struggled tow'rds
Some sense; and still in the last chords
The music seemed to sing wild words.

The Bride's Prelude.

"My shame possessed me in the light
    And pageant, till I swooned.
But from that hour I put my shame
From me, and cast it over them
By God's command and in God's name

"For my child's bitter sake.　O thou
    Once felt against my heart
With longing of the eyes,—a pain
Since to my heart for ever,—then
Beheld not, and not felt again!"

She scarcely paused, continuing: —
    "That year drooped weak in March;
And April, finding the streams dry,
Choked, with no rain, in dust: the sky
Shall not be fainter this July.

"Men sickened; beasts lay without strength,
    The year died in the land.
But I, already desolate,
Said merely, sitting down to wait,—
'The seasons change and Time wears late.'

"For I had my hard secret told,
    In secret, to a priest;
With him I communed; and he said
The world's soul, for its sins, was sped,
And the sun's courses numberèd.

"The year slid like a corpse afloat:
    None trafficked,—who had bread
Did eat.　That year our legions, come
Thinned from the place of war, at home
Found busier death, more burdensome.

The Bride's Prelude.

"Tidings and rumours came with them,
  The first for months.   The chiefs
Sat daily at our board, and in
· Their speech were names of friend and kin;
One day they spoke of Urscelyn.

"The words were light, among the rest:
  Quick glance my brothers sent
To sift the speech; and I, struck through,
Sat sick and giddy in full view:
Yet did none gaze, so many knew.

"Because in the beginning, much
  Had caught abroad, through them
That heard my clamour on the coast:
But two were hanged; and then the most
Held silence wisdom, as thou know'st.

"That year the convent yielded thee
  Back to our home; and thou
Then knew'st not how I shuddered cold
To kiss thee, seeming to enfold
To my changed heart myself of old.

"Then there was showing thee the house,
  So many rooms and doors;
Thinking the while how thou would'st start
If once I flung the doors apart
Of one dull chamber in my heart.

"And yet I longed to open it;
  And often in that year
Of plague and want, when side by side
We 've knelt to pray with them that died,
My prayer was, ' Show her what I hide!' "

END OF PART I.

THE BLESSED DAMOZEL.

THREE versions of this poem exist; that published in *The Germ* in 1850; the one in *The Oxford and Cambridge Magazine* in 1856, and the one in the *Poems of 1870*. Although the changes almost invariably improved the poem, the older readings were, as Mr. Swinburne has said, often so good that no one without Rossetti's "insatiable passion for the best" would have been dissatisfied with them. To afford the reader opportunity for satisfactory comparison, the text as it appeared in *The Germ* has been reprinted in the notes in full. The slighter variations in *The Oxford and Cambridge Magazine* are given in notes to the later version. Certainly none of Rossetti's poems shows more the effect of the *labor limæ* to which he was so much addicted.

The theme of *The Blessed Damozel* was suggested by Poe's *Raven*, that poem and others by Poe forming, to use Mr. William Rossetti's expression, "a deep well of delight" to Rossetti during his early years. "I saw," he said, "that Poe had done the utmost it was possible to do with the grief of the lover on earth, and I determined to reverse the conditions, and give utterance to the yearning of the loved one in heaven."

The poem was written in 1847 before Rossetti was nineteen years old. The first picture painted by him in illustration of it is dated more than a quarter of a century later.

THE BLESSED DAMOZEL.

(As published in " The Germ.")

THE blessed Damozel leaned out
  From the gold bar of Heaven:
Her blue grave eyes were deeper much
  Than a deep water, even.
She had three lilies in her hand,
  And the stars in her hair were seven.

Her robe, ungirt from clasp to hem,
  No wrought flowers did adorn,
But a white rose of Mary's gift,
  On the neck meetly worn;
And her hair, lying down her back,
  Was yellow like ripe corn.

Herseemed she scarce had been a day
  One of God's choristers;
The wonder was not yet quite gone
  From that still look of her's;
Albeit to them she left, her day
  Had counted as ten years.

(To *one* it is ten years of years:
  . . . Yet now, here in this place,
Surely she leaned o'er me,—her hair
  Fell all about my face. . . .
Nothing: the Autumn-fall of leaves.
  The whole year sets a pace.)

It was the terrace of God's house
  That she was standing on,—
By God built over the sheer depth
  In which Space is begun;

The Blessed Damozel

So high, that looking downward thence
   She could scarce see the sun.

It lies from Heaven across the flood
   Of ether, as a bridge.
Beneath, the tides of day and night
   With flame and blackness ridge
The void, as low as where this earth
   Spins like a fretful midge.

But in those tracts, with her, it was
   The peace of utter light
And silence.   For no breeze may stir
   Along the steady flight
Of seraphim; no echo there,
   Beyond all depth or height.

Heard hardly, some of her new friends,
   Playing at holy games,
Spake, gentle-mouthed, among themselves,
   Their virginal chaste names;
And the souls mounting up to God,
   Went by her like thin flames.

And still she bowed herself, and stooped
   Into the vast waste calm;
Till her bosom's pressure must have made
   The bar she leaned on warm,
And the lilies lay as if asleep
   Along her bended arm.

From the fixt lull of heaven, she saw
   Time, like a pulse, shake fierce
Through all the worlds.   Her gaze still strove,
   In that steep gulph, to pierce
The swarm: and then she spake, as when
   The stars sang in their spheres.

"I wish that he were come to me,
   For he will come," she said.

The Blessed Damozel

" Yea, verily; when he is come
   We will do thus and thus:
Till this my vigil seem quite strange
   And almost fabulous;
We two will live at once, one life ;
   And peace shall be with us."

She gazed and listened and then said,
   Less sad of speech than mild;
" All this is when he comes."   She ceased:
   The light thrilled past her, filled
With Angels, in strong level lapse.
   Her eyes prayed, and she smiled.

(I saw her smile.)   But soon their flight
   Was vague 'mid the poised spheres.
And then she cast her arms along
   The golden barriers,
And laid her face between her hands,
   And wept.   (I heard her tears.)

The Blessed Damozel. 1879.

The Blind Damozel. 1879.

THE BLESSED DAMOZEL.

(With Four Illustrations.)

THE blessed damozel leaned out
  From the gold bar of Heaven;
Her eyes were deeper than the depth
  Of waters stilled at even ¹;
She had three lilies in her hand,
  And the stars in her hair were seven.

Her robe, ungirt from clasp to hem,
  No wrought flowers did adorn,
But a white rose of Mary's gift,
  For service meetly worn;
Her hair that lay along her back ²
  Was yellow like ripe corn.

Herseemed she scarce had been a day
  One of God's choristers;
The wonder was not yet quite gone
  From that still look of hers;
Albeit, to them she left, her day
  Had counted as ten years.

(To one, it is ten years of years.
  . . . Yet now, and in this place,
Surely she leaned o'er me — her hair
  Fell all about my face. . . .
Nothing: the autumn-fall of leaves.
  The whole year sets apace.)

The Blessed Damozel

It was the rampart of God's house
  That she was standing on;
By God built over the sheer depth
  The which is Space begun;
So high, that looking downward thence
  She scarce could see the sun.

It lies in Heaven, across the flood
  Of ether, as a bridge.
Beneath, the tides of day and night
  With flame and darkness ridge
The void, as low as where this earth
  Spins like a fretful midge.

Around her, lovers, newly met
  'Mid deathless love's acclaims,
Spoke evermore among themselves
  Their heart-remembered names ';
And the souls mounting up to God
  Went by her like thin flames.

And still she bowed herself and stooped
  Out of the circling charm ';
Until her bosom must have made
  The bar she leaned on warm,
And the lilies lay as if asleep
  Along her bended arm.

From the fixed place of Heaven she saw
  Time like a pulse shake fierce
Through all the worlds.   Her gaze still strove
  Within the gulf to pierce
Its path; and now she spoke as when
  The stars sang in their spheres.

The Blessed Damozel

The sun was gone now; the curled moon
   Was like a little feather
Fluttering far down the gulf; and now
   She spoke through the still weather.
Her voice was like the voice the stars
   Had when they sang together.'

(Ah sweet! Even now, in that bird's song,
   Strove not her accents there,
Fain to be hearkened? When those bells
   Possessed the mid-day air,
Strove not her steps to reach my side
   Down all the echoing stair?) '

"I wish that he were come to me,
   For he will come," she said.
"Have I not prayed in Heaven?— on earth,
   Lord, Lord, has he not pray'd?
Are not two prayers a perfect strength?
   And shall I feel afraid?

"When round his head the aureole clings,
   And he is clothed in white,
I 'll take his hand and go with him
   To the deep wells of light;
As unto a stream we will step down,'
   And bathe there in God's sight.

"We two will stand beside that shrine,
   Occult, withheld, untrod,
Whose lamps are stirred continually
   With prayer sent up to God;
And see our old prayers, granted, melt
   Each like a little cloud.

The Blessed Damozel

" We two will lie i' the shadow of
   That living mystic tree
Within whose secret growth the Dove
   Is sometimes felt to be,
While every leaf that His plumes touch
   Saith His Name audibly.

" And I myself will teach to him,
   I myself, lying so,
The songs I sing here; which his voice
   Shall pause in, hushed and slow,
And find some knowledge at each pause,
   Or some new thing to know."

(Alas! we two, we two, thou say'st!
   Yea, one wast thou with me
That once of old.   But shall God lift
   To endless unity
The soul whose likeness with thy soul
   Was but its love for thee ?) '

" We two," she said, " will seek the groves
   Where the lady Mary is,
With her five handmaidens, whose names
   Are five sweet symphonies,
Cecily, Gertrude, Magdalen,
   Margaret and Rosalys.

" Circlewise sit they, with bound locks
   And foreheads garlanded;
Into the fine cloth white like flame
   Weaving the golden thread,
To fashion the birth-robes for them
   Who are just born, being dead.

The Blessed Damozel.

"He shall fear, haply, and be dumb:
  Then will I lay my cheek
To his, and tell about our love,
  Not once abashed or weak:
And the dear Mother will approve
  My pride, and let me speak.

"Herself shall bring us, hand in hand,
  To Him round whom all souls
Kneel, the clear-ranged unnumbered heads'
  Bowed with their aureoles:
And angels meeting us shall sing
  To their citherns and citoles.

"There will I ask of Christ the Lord
  Thus much for him and me:—
Only to live as once on earth
  With Love,— only to be,'°
As then awhile, for ever now
  Together, I and he."

She gazed and listened and then said,
  Less sad of speech than mild,—
"All this is when he comes."   She ceased.
  The light thrilled towards her, fill'd"
With angels in strong level flight.
  Her eyes prayed, and she smil'd.

(I saw her smile.)   But soon their path
  Was vague and distant spheres:
And then she cast her arms along'²
  The golden barriers,
And laid her face between her hands,
  And wept.   (I heard her tears.)

MY SISTER'S SLEEP.

IT is interesting to note that what would now be called the "Pre-Raphaelite detail" of this poem, written no later than 1847, antedates the formation of the Pre-Raphaelite Brotherhood and indicates the tendency of Rossetti's mind toward specific pictorial images before he had met any of the men who were afterward to belong to that famous little band, in whose literary organ, *The Germ*, the poem was first printed. When it came to be reprinted among Rossetti's collected *Poems*, he took its defects very seriously and made a quantity of emendations concerning which he was at great pains to consult his family and friends. The version that appeared in *The Germ* is reprinted in the Notes as a record of Rossetti's fastidious care in bettering his work where he saw the possibility of doing so.

SONGS OF ONE HOUSEHOLD.

NO. I.

MY SISTER'S SLEEP.

(As published in "The Germ.")

SHE fell asleep on Christmas Eve,
   Upon her eyes' most patient calms
   The lids were shut; her uplaid arms
Covered her bosom, I believe.

Our mother, who had leaned all day
   Over the bed from chime to chime,
   Then raised herself for the first time,
And as she sat her down, did pray.

Her little work-table was spread
   With work to finish. For the glare
   Made by her candle, she had care
To work some distance from the bed.

Without, there was a good moon up,
   Which left its shadows far within;
   The depth of light that it was in
Seemed hollow like an altar-cup.

Through the small room, with subtle sound
   Of flame, by vents the fireshine drove
   And reddened. In its dim alcove
The mirror shed a clearness round.

I had been sitting up some nights,
   And my tir'd mind felt weak and blank;

My Sister's Sleep.

Like a sharp strengthening wine, it drank
The stillness and the broken lights.

Silence was speaking at my side
   With an exceedingly clear voice;
   I knew the calm as of a choice
Made in God for me, to abide.

I said, " Full knowledge does not grieve:
   This which upon my spirit dwells
   Perhaps would have been sorrow else:
But I am glad 't is Christmas Eve."

Twelve struck.   That sound which all the years
   Hear in each hour, crept off; and then
   The ruffled silence spread again,
Like water that a pebble stirs.

Our mother rose from where she sat:
   Her needles, as she laid them down,
   Met lightly, and her silken gown
Settled: no other noise than that.

" Glory unto the Newly Born! "
   So as said angels, she did say;
   Because we were in Christmas-day,
Though it would still be long till dawn.

She stood a moment with her hands
   Kept in each other, praying much;
   A moment that the soul may touch
But the heart only understands.

Almost unwittingly, my mind
   Repeated her words after her;
   Perhaps tho' my lips did not stir;
It was scarce thought, or cause assign'd.

Just then in the room over us
   There was a pushing back of chairs,
   As some who had sat unawares
So late, now heard the hour, and rose.

My Sister's Sleep.

Anxious, with softly stepping haste,
   Our mother went where Margaret lay,
   Fearing the sounds o'erhead—should they
Have broken her long-watched for rest!

She stooped an instant, calm, and turned;
   But suddenly turned back again;
   And all her features seemed in pain
With woe, and her eyes gazed and yearned.

For my part, I but hid my face,
   And held my breath, and spake no word:
   There was none spoken; but *I heard
The silence* for a little space.

Our mother bowed herself and wept.
   And both my arms fell, and I said:
   "God knows I knew that she was dead."
And there, all white, my sister slept.

Then kneeling, upon Christmas morn
   A little after twelve o'clock
We said, ere the first quarter struck,
   "Christ's blessing on the newly born!"

MY SISTER'S SLEEP.[1]

SHE fell asleep on Christmas Eve.
  At length the long-ungranted shade
  Of weary eyelids overweigh'd
The pain nought else might yet relieve.

Our mother, who had leaned all day
  Over the bed from chime to chime,
  Then raised herself for the first time,
And as she sat her down, did pray.

Her little work-table was spread
  With work to finish.   For the glare
  Made by her candle, she had care
To work some distance from the bed.

Without, there was a cold moon up,
  Of winter radiance sheer and thin;
  The hollow halo it was in
Was like an icy crystal cup.

Through the small room, with subtle sound
  Of flame, by vents the fireshine drove
  And reddened.   In its dim alcove
The mirror shed a clearness round.

I had been sitting up some nights,
  And my tired mind felt weak and blank;
  Like a sharp strengthening wine it drank
The stillness and the broken lights.

My Sister's Sleep.

Twelve struck.   That sound, by dwindling years
  Heard in each hour, crept off ; and then
The ruffled silence spread again,
  Like water that a pebble stirs.

Our mother rose from where she sat:
  Her needles, as she laid them down,
  Met lightly, and her silken gown
Settled: no other noise than that.

"Glory unto the Newly Born!"
  So, as said angels, she did say;
  Because we were in Christmas Day,
Though it would still be long till morn.

Just then in the room over us
  There was a pushing back of chairs,
  As some who had sat unawares
So late, now heard the hour, and rose.

With anxious softly-stepping haste
  Our mother went where Margaret lay,
  Fearing the sounds o'erhead — should they
Have broken her long watched-for rest!

She stopped an instant, calm, and turned;
  But suddenly turned back again;
  And all her features seemed in pain
With woe, and her eyes gazed and yearned.

For my part, I but hid my face,
  And held my breath, and spoke no word.
  There was none spoken; but I heard
The silence for a little space.

My Sister's Sleep.

Our mother bowed herself and wept:
  And both my arms fell, and I said,
   "God knows I knew that she was dead."
And there, all white, my sister slept.

Then kneeling, upon Christmas morn
  A little after twelve o'clock,
  We said, ere the first quarter struck,
"Christ's blessing on the newly born!"

THE PORTRAIT.

The Portrait was written in 1847 for a little manuscript magazine called *Hotch Potch* that flourished in the Rossetti family for a brief period, members of the family contributing to it. Rossetti considered the poem unworthy for publication in *The Germ,* and before it found its way into the volume of *Poems* of 1870 it was to a considerable extent rewritten. When, before his wife's death, he contemplated publishing his poems, he wrote to William Allingham, with whom he was in consultation, concerning poems to be included or omitted:

"The one of any length I most thought of omitting myself is *The Portrait,* which is rather spoon-meat; but this, I see, you do not name, and perhaps I may leave it."

Before the volume of 1881 appeared a change was made in the second stanza at the suggestion of Hall Caine, who found the original reading somewhat puzzling. The fifth line originally ran:

Yet this of all love's perfect prize.

The poem has been described as referring to Rossetti's wife; but the date of its composition precludes any such reference. Very possibly, of course, in his later additions to it he had his wife in mind.

THE PORTRAIT.[1]

THIS is her picture as she was:
   It seems a thing to wonder on,
As though mine image in the glass
   Should tarry when myself am gone.
I gaze until she seems to stir,—
Until mine eyes almost aver
  · That now, even now, the sweet lips part
   To breathe the words of the sweet heart:—
And yet the earth is over her.

Alas! even such the thin-drawn ray
   That makes the prison-depths more rude,—
The drip of water night and day
   Giving a tongue to solitude.
Yet only this, of love's whole prize,
Remains; save what in mournful guise
   Takes counsel with my soul alone,—
   Save what is secret and unknown,
Below the earth, above the skies.

In painting her I shrined her face
   'Mid mystic trees, where light falls in
Hardly at all; a covert place
   Where you might think to find a din
Of doubtful talk, and a live flame
Wandering, and many a shape whose name
   Not itself knoweth, and old dew,
   And your own footsteps meeting you,
And all things going as they came.

Study for " The Blessed Damozel."

Red chalk. 1875.

The Portrait.

A deep dim wood; and there she stands
   As in that wood that day: for so
Was the still movement of her hands
   And such the pure line's gracious flow.
And passing fair the type must seem,
Unknown the presence and the dream.
   'T is she: though of herself, alas!
   Less than her shadow on the grass
Or than her image in the stream.

That day we met there, I and she
   One with the other all alone;
And we were blithe; yet memory
   Saddens those hours, as when the moon
Looks upon daylight.   And with her
I stooped to drink the spring-water,
   Athirst where other waters sprang:
   And where the echo is, she sang,—
My soul another echo there.

But when that hour my soul won strength
   For words whose silence wastes and kills,
Dull raindrops smote us, and at length
   Thundered the heat within the hills.
That eve I spoke those words again
Beside the pelted window-pane;
   And there she hearkened what I said,
   With under-glances that surveyed
The empty pastures blind with rain.

Next day the memories of these things,
   Like leaves through which a bird has flown
Still vibrated with Love's warm wings;
   Till I must make them all my own

The Portrait.

And paint this picture.   So, 'twixt ease
Of talk and sweet long silences,
   She stood among the plants in bloom
   At windows of a summer room,
To feign the shadow of the trees.

And as I wrought, while all above
   And all around was fragrant air,
In the sick burthen of my love
   It seemed each sun-thrilled blossom there
Beat like a heart among the leaves.
O heart that never beats nor heaves,
   In that one darkness lying still,
   What now to thee my love's great will
Or the fine web the sunshine weaves?

For now doth daylight disavow
   Those days—nought left to see or hear.
Only in solemn whispers now
   At night-time these things reach mine ear;
When the leaf-shadows at a breath
Shrink in the road, and all the heath,
   Forest and water, far and wide,
   In limpid starlight glorified,
Lie like the mystery of death.

Last night at last I could have slept,
   And yet delayed my sleep till dawn,
Still wandering.   Then it was I wept:
   For unawares I came upon
Those glades where once she walked with me:
And as I stood there suddenly,
   All wan with traversing the night,
   Upon the desolate verge of light
Yearned loud the iron-bosomed sea.

The Portrait.

Even so, where Heaven holds breath and hears
  The beating heart of Love's own breast,—
Where round the secret of all spheres
  All angels lay their wings to rest,—
How shall my soul stand rapt and awed,
When, by the new birth borne abroad
  Throughout the music of the suns,
  It enters in her soul at once
And knows the silence there for God!

Here with her face doth memory sit
  Meanwhile, and wait the day's decline,
Till other eyes shall look from it,
  Eyes of the spirit's Palestine,
Even than the old gaze tenderer:
While hopes and aims long lost with her
  Stand round her image side by side
  Like tombs of pilgrims that have died
About the Holy Sepulchre.

JENNY.

THE first version of *Jenny* was written in 1847. In this early form it had, according to Mr. William Rossetti, "none of that slight framework of incident now belonging to the poem." It was brought to completion eleven years later, and the manuscript, together with the manuscript copies of many other poems written by Rossetti, was buried in his wife's coffin in 1862. It was recovered in 1869 and revised prior to its publication in the volume of 1870. Upon its appearance in that volume Rossetti wrote to his aunt:

"I felt uncertain whether you would be pleased with it. I am not ashamed of having written it (indeed I assure you that I would never have written it if I thought it unfit to be read with good results); but I feared it might startle you somewhat, and so put off sending you the book. I now do so by this post, and hope that some, if not all of the pieces may be quite to your taste. Indeed, I hope that even *Jenny* may be so, for my mother likes it on the whole the best in the volume, after some consideration."

Later he said to Hall Caine: "As to *Jenny*, it is a sermon, nothing less."

In 1860 *Jenny* was sent to Ruskin for publication in the *Cornhill;* but was returned with a letter of sharp criticism. He objected, among other things, to the rhyming of "Jenny" with "guinea," but he chiefly disapproved of the "cold-blooded" temper in which the philosopher of the poem conducts his meditations.

JENNY.

*Vengeance of Jenny's case! Fie on her! Never name
her, child!*—(Mrs. Quickly.)

LAZY laughing languid Jenny,
Fond of a kiss and fond of a guinea,
Whose head upon my knee to-night
Rests for a while, as if grown light
With all our dances and the sound
To which the wild tunes spun you round:
Fair Jenny mine, the thoughtless queen
Of kisses which the blush between
Could hardly make much daintier;
Whose eyes are as blue skies, whose hair
Is countless gold incomparable:
Fresh flower, scarce touched with signs that tell
Of Love's exuberant hotbed:—Nay,
Poor flower left torn since yesterday
Until to-morrow leave you bare;
Poor handful of bright spring-water
Flung in the whirlpool's shrieking face;
Poor shameful Jenny, full of grace
Thus with your head upon my knee;—
Whose person or whose purse may be
The lodestar of your reverie?

This room of yours, my Jenny, looks
A change from mine so full of books,

Jenny.

Whose serried ranks hold fast, forsooth,
So many captive hours of youth,—
The hours they thieve from day and night
To make one's cherished work come right,
And leave it wrong for all their theft,
Even as to-night my work was left:
Until I vowed that since my brain
And eyes of dancing seemed so fain,
My feet should have some dancing too:—
And thus it was I met with you.
Well, I suppose 't was hard to part,
For here I am.   And now, sweetheart,
You seem too tired to get to bed.

   It was a careless life I led
When rooms like this were scarce so strange
Not long ago.   What breeds the change,—
The many aims or the few years?
Because to-night it all appears
Something I do not know again.

   The cloud 's not danced out of my brain,—
The cloud that made it turn and swim
While hour by hour the books grew dim.
Why, Jenny, as I watch you there,—
For all your wealth of loosened hair,
Your silk ungirdled and unlac'd
And warm sweets open to the waist,
All golden in the lamplight's gleam,—
You know not what a book you seem,
Half-read by lightning in a dream!
How should you know, my Jenny?   Nay,
And I should be ashamed to say:—
Poor beauty, so well worth a kiss!
But while my thought runs on like this

Jenny.

With wasteful whims more than enough,
I wonder what you 're thinking of.

   If of myself you think at all,
What is the thought ? — conjectural
On sorry matters best unsolved ?—
Or inly is each grace revolved
To fit me with a lure ? — or (sad
To think!) perhaps you 're merely glad
That I 'm not drunk or ruffianly
And let you rest upon my knee.

   For sometimes, were the truth confess'd,
You 're thankful for a little rest, —
Glad from the crush to rest within,
From the heart-sickness and the din
Where envy's voice at virtue's pitch
Mocks you because your gown is rich;
And from the pale girl's dumb rebuke,
Whose ill-clad grace and toil-worn look
Proclaim the strength that keeps her weak,
And other nights than yours bespeak;
And from the wise unchildish elf,
To schoolmate lesser than himself
Pointing you out, what thing you are:—
Yes, from the daily jeer and jar,
From shame and shame 's outbraving too,
Is rest not sometimes sweet to you ?—
But most from the hatefulness of man,
Who spares not to end what he began,
Whose acts are ill and his speech ill,
Who, having used you at his will,
Thrusts you aside, as when I dine
I serve the dishes and the wine.

Jenny.

Well, handsome Jenny mine, sit up:
I've filled our glasses, let us sup,
And do not let me think of you,
Lest shame of yours suffice for two.
What, still so tired? Well, well then, keep
Your head there, so you do not sleep;
But that the weariness may pass
And leave you merry, take this glass,
Ah! lazy lily hand, more bless'd
If ne'er in rings it had been dress'd
Nor ever by a glove conceal'd!

Behold the lilies of the field,
They toil not neither do they spin;
(So doth the ancient text begin,—
Not of such rest as one of these
Can share.) Another rest and ease
Along each summer-sated path
From its new lord the garden hath,
Than that whose spring in blessings ran
Which praised the bounteous husbandman,
Ere yet, in days of hankering breath,
The lilies sickened unto death.

What, Jenny, are your lilies dead?
Aye, and the snow-white leaves are spread
Like winter on the garden-bed.
But you had roses left in May,—
They were not gone too. Jenny, nay,
But must your roses die, and those
Their purfled buds that should unclose?
Even so; the leaves are curled apart,
Still red as from the broken heart,
And here's the naked stem of thorns.

Jenny.

Nay, nay, mere words.   Here nothing warns
As yet of winter.   Sickness here
Or want alone could waken fear,—
Nothing but passion wrings a tear.
Except when there may rise unsought
Haply at times a passing thought
Of the old days which seem to be
Much older than any history
That is written in any book;
When she would lie in fields and look
Along the ground through the blown grass,
And wonder where the city was,
Far out of sight, whose broil and bale
They told her then for a child's tale.

Jenny, you know the city now.
A child can tell the tale there, how
Some things which are not yet enroll'd
In market-lists are bought and sold
Even till the early Sunday light,
When Saturday night is market-night
Everywhere, be it dry or wet,
And market-night in the Haymarket.
Our learned London children know,
Poor Jenny, all your pride and woe;
Have seen your lifted silken skirt
Advertise dainties through the dirt;
Have seen your coach-wheels splash rebuke
On virtue; and have learned your look
When, wealth and health slipped past, you stare
Along the streets alone, and there,
Round the long park, across the bridge,
The cold lamps at the pavement's edge

Jenny.

Wind on together and apart,
A fiery serpent for your heart.

Let the thoughts pass, an empty cloud!
Suppose I were to think aloud,—
What if to her all this were said?
Why, as a volume seldom read
Being opened halfway shuts again,
So might the pages of her brain
Be parted at such words, and thence
Close back upon the dusty sense.
For is there hue or shape defin'd
In Jenny's desecrated mind,
Where all contagious currents meet,
A Lethe of the middle street?
Nay, it reflects not any face,
Nor sound is in its sluggish pace,
But as they coil those eddies clot,
And night and day remember not.

Why, Jenny, you're asleep at last!
Asleep, poor Jenny, hard and fast,—
So young and soft and tired; so fair,
With chin thus nestled in your hair,
Mouth quiet, eyelids almost blue
As if some sky of dreams shone through!

Just as another woman sleeps!
Enough to throw one's thoughts in heaps
Of doubt and horror,—what to say
Or think,—this awful secret sway,
The potter's power over the clay!
Of the same lump (it has been said)
For honour and dishonour made,
Two sister vessels.   Here is one.

Jenny.

My cousin Nell is fond of fun,
And fond of dress, and change, and praise,
So mere a woman in her ways:
And if her sweet eyes rich in youth
Are like her lips that tell the truth,
My cousin Nell is fond of love.
And she 's the girl I 'm proudest of.
Who does not prize her, guard her well?
The love of change, in cousin Nell,
Shall find the best and hold it dear:
The unconquered mirth turn quieter
Not through her own, through others' woe:
The conscious pride of beauty glow
Beside another's pride in her,
One little part of all they share.
For Love himself shall ripen these
In a kind soil to just increase
Through years of fertilising peace.

Of the same lump (as it is said)
For honour and dishonour made,
Two sister vessels.   Here is one.

It makes a goblin of the sun.

So pure,—so fall'n!   How dare to think
Of the first common kindred link?
Yet, Jenny, till the world shall burn
It seems that all things take their turn;
And who shall say but this fair tree
May need, in changes that may be,
Your children's children's charity?
Scorned then, no doubt, as you are scorn'd!
Shall no man hold his pride forewarn'd
Till in the end, the Day of Days,

Jenny.

At Judgment, one of his own race,
As frail and lost as you, shall rise,—
His daughter, with his mother's eyes?

How Jenny's clock ticks on the shelf!
Might not the dial scorn itself
That has such hours to register?
Yet as to me, even so to her
Are golden sun and silver moon,
In daily largesse of earth's boon,
Counted for life-coins to one tune.
And if, as blindfold fates are toss'd,
Through some one man this life be lost,
Shall soul not somehow pay for soul?

Fair shines the gilded aureole
In which our highest painters place
Some living woman's simple face.
And the stilled features thus descried
As Jenny's long throat droops aside,—
The shadows where the cheeks are thin,
And pure wide curve from ear to chin,—
With Raffael's, Leonardo's hand '
To show them to men's souls, might stand,
Whole ages long, the whole world through,
For preachings of what God can do.
What has man done here? How atone,
Great God, for this which man has done?
And for the body and soul which by
Man's pitiless doom must now comply
With lifelong hell, what lullaby
Of sweet forgetful second birth
Remains? All dark. No sign on earth

Jenny.

What measure of God's rest endows
The many mansions of His house.

  If but a woman's heart might see
Such erring heart unerringly
For once!   But that can never be.

  Like a rose shut in a book
In which pure women may not look,
For its base pages claim control
To crush the flower within the soul;
Where through each dead rose-leaf that clings,
Pale as transparent Psyche-wings,
To the vile text, are traced such things
As might make lady's cheek indeed
More than a living rose to read;
So nought save foolish foulness may
Watch with hard eyes the sure decay;
And so the life-blood of this rose,
Puddled with shameful knowledge, flows
Through leaves no chaste hand may unclose:
Yet still it keeps such faded show
Of when 't was gathered long ago,
That the crushed petals' lovely grain,
The sweetness of the sanguine stain,
Seen of a woman's eyes, must make
Her pitiful heart, so prone to ache,
Love roses better for its sake:—
Only that this can never be:—
Even so unto her sex is she.

  Yet, Jenny, looking long at you,
The woman almost fades from view.
A cipher of man's changeless sum
Of lust, past, present, and to come,

Jenny.

Is left.   A riddle that one shrinks
To challenge from the scornful sphinx.

   Like a toad within a stone
Seated while Time crumbles on;
Which sits there since the earth was curs'd
For Man's transgression at the first;
Which, living through all centuries,
Not once has seen the sun arise;
Whose life, to its cold circle charmed,
The earth's whole summers have not warmed;
Which always—whitherso the stone
Be flung—sits there, deaf, blind, alone;—
Aye, and shall not be driven out
Till that which shuts him round about
Break at the very Master's stroke,
And the dust thereof vanish as smoke,
And the seed of Man vanish as dust:—
Even so within this world is Lust.

   Come, come, what use in thoughts like this?
Poor little Jenny, good to kiss,—
You 'd not believe by what strange roads
Thought travels, when your beauty goads
A man to-night to think of toads!
Jenny, wake up . . . Why, there 's the dawn!

   And there 's an early waggon drawn
To market, and some sheep that jog
Bleating before a barking dog;
And the old streets come peering through
Another night that London knew;
And all as ghostlike as the lamps.

Jenny.

So on the wings of day decamps
My last night's frolic.   Glooms begin
To shiver off as lights creep in
Past the gauze curtains half drawn-to,
And the lamp's doubled shade grows blue,—
Your lamp, my Jenny, kept alight,
Like a wise virgin's, all one night!
And in the alcove coolly spread
Glimmers with dawn your empty bed;
And yonder your fair face I see
Reflected lying on my knee,
Where teems with first foreshadowings
Your pier-glass scrawled with diamond rings:
And on your bosom all night worn [3]
Yesterday's rose now droops forlorn,
But dies not yet this summer morn.

And now without, as if some word
Had called upon them that they heard,
The London sparrows far and nigh
Clamour together suddenly;
And Jenny's cage-bird grown awake
Here in their song his part must take,
Because here too the day doth break.

And somehow in myself the dawn
Among stirred clouds and veils withdrawn
Strikes greyly on her.   Let her sleep.
But will it wake her if I heap
These cushions thus beneath her head
Where my knee was?   No,—there 's your bed,
My Jenny, while you dream.   And there
I lay among your golden hair
Perhaps the subject of your dreams,

Jenny.

These golden coins.

             For still one deems
That Jenny's flattering sleep confers
New magic on the magic purse,—
Grim web, how clogged with shrivelled flies!
Between the threads fine fumes arise
And shape their pictures in the brain.
There roll no streets in glare and rain,
Nor flagrant man-swine whets his tusk;
But delicately sighs in musk
The homage of the dim boudoir;
Or like a palpitating star
Thrilled into song, the opera-night
Breathes faint in the quick pulse of light;
Or at the carriage-window shine
Rich wares for choice; or, free to dine,
Whirls through its hour of health (divine
For her) the concourse of the Park.
And though in the discounted dark
Her functions there and here are one,
Beneath the lamps and in the sun
There reigns at least the acknowledged belle
Apparelled beyond parallel.
Ah Jenny, yes, we know your dreams.

   For even the Paphian Venus seems
A goddess o'er the realms of love,
When silver-shrined in shadowy grove:
Aye, or let offerings nicely plac'd
But hide Priapus to the waist,
And whoso looks on him shall see
An eligible deity.

   Why, Jenny, waking here alone

Jenny.

May help you to remember one,
Though all the memory 's long outworn
Of many a double-pillowed morn.
I think I see you when you wake,
And rub your eyes for me, and shake
My gold, in rising, from your hair,
A Danaë for a moment there.

Jenny, my love rang true! for still
Love at first sight is vague, until
That tinkling makes him audible.

And must I mock you to the last,
Ashamed of my own shame,—aghast
Because some thoughts not born amiss
Rose at a poor fair face like this?
Well, of such thoughts so much I know:
In my life, as in hers, they show,
By a far gleam which I may near,
A dark path I can strive to clear.

Only one kiss.   Good-bye, my dear.

THE LADY'S LAMENT.

(1848.)

NEVER happy any more!
Aye, turn the saying o'er and o'er,
It says but what it said before,
And heart and life are just as sore.
The wet leaves blow aslant the floor
In the rain through the open door.
      No, no more.

Never happy any more!
The eyes are weary and give o'er,
But still the soul weeps as before.
And always must each one deplore
Each once, nor bear what others bore?
This is now as it was of yore.
      No, no more.

Never happy any more!
Is it not but a sorry lore
That says, "Take strength, the worst is o'er."
Shall the stars seem as heretofore?
The day wears on more and more —
While I was weeping the day wore.
      No, no more.

Never happy any more!
In the cold behind the door

The Lady's Lament.

That was the dial striking four:
One for joy the past hours bore,
Two for hope and will cast o'er,
One for the naked dark before.
       No, no more.

Never happy any more!
Put the light out, shut the door,
Sweep the wet leaves from the floor.
Even thus Fate's hand has swept her floor,
Even thus Love's hand has shut the door
Through which his warm feet passed of yore.
Shall it be opened any more ?
       No, no, no more.

Made for the press in the by-request of
" The Blue Dragon."

AUTUMN SONG.[1]

(1848.)

KNOW'ST thou not at the fall of the leaf
How the heart feels a languid grief
    Laid on it for a covering,
    And how sleep seems a goodly thing
In Autumn at the fall of the leaf?

And how the swift beat of the brain
Falters because it is in vain,
    In Autumn at the fall of the leaf
    Knowest thou not? and how the chief
Of joys seems—not to suffer pain?

Know'st thou not at the fall of the leaf
How the soul feels like a dried sheaf
    Bound up at length for harvesting,
    And how death seems a comely thing
In Autumn at the fall of the leaf?

MARY'S GIRLHOOD.

THESE two sonnets are notable as having been written for Rossetti's first exhibited picture, painted in 1848, and hung in the Free Exhibition of 1849.

The first of the two sonnets appeared in the catalogue of the exhibition, and was greatly admired by Sir Theodore Martin who characterised it as "one of the finest in the language," and distributed copies of it among his friends. Both sonnets were printed on a slip of gilt paper for the frame of the picture, the first expressing the general intention of the artist and the second interpreting the special symbols. The figures in the picture are all portraits and good likenesses. The St. Joachim, training up a vine in the background, was painted from a man named Williams, a "jobbing man" employed in the Rossetti family to black boots, etc. He entertained a special predilection for Dante Gabriel Rossetti. The St. Anna was painted from Rossetti's mother, then forty-eight years old. The Virgin is a likeness of Christina except that in the picture the hair is golden instead of dark brown, the colour of Christina's. The little angel was first painted from a young sister of Woolner, the sculptor, but later repainted from a model. Mr. F. G. Stephens writes of the picture in his monograph on Rossetti: "A little flat and gray, and rather thin in painting, it is most carefully drawn and soundly modelled, rich in good and pure colouring; and in the brooding, dreamy pathos, full of reverence and yet unconscious of the time to come, which the Virgin's still and chaste face expresses, there is a vein of poetry, the freshest and most profound."

The picture was promptly sold for £80, the price put upon it by the young painter. It was also praised by the critics who had not yet opened their eyes to the sins of the Pre-Raphaelite Brotherhood. The first sonnet is printed in Rossetti's *Letters* in the following form:

> This is that Blessed Mary, pre-elect
>> God's Virgin.   Gone is a great while since she
>> Dwelt thus in Nazareth of Galilee.
> Loving she was, with temperate respect;
> A profound simpleness of intellect
>> Was hers, and extreme patience.   From the knee
>> Faithful and hopeful; wise in charity;
> Strong in grave peace; in duty circumspect.
> Thus held she through her girlhood; as it were
>> An angel-watered lily that near God
>>> Grows and is quiet.   Till one dawn, at home
> She woke in her white bed, and had no fear
>> At all, yet wept for a brief period;
>>> Because the fullness of the time was come.

Rossetti was ever punctilious concerning plagiarism, and a notable instance of his sensitiveness on the subject is his explanation to his brother that he is free to write "an angel-watered lily" although in one of his translations from the Italian poet Mamiani he uses the expression, "an angel-watered plant," since the phrase was not in Mamiani at all but was an addition of his own.

MARY'S GIRLHOOD.

(For a picture. 1848.)

I.

THIS is that blessed Mary, pre-elect
  God's Virgin.   Gone is a great while, and she
  Dwelt young in Nazareth of Galilee.
Unto God's will she brought devout respect,
Profound simplicity of intellect,
  And supreme patience.   From her mother's knee
  Faithful and hopeful; wise in charity;
Strong in grave peace; in pity circumspect.

So held she through her girlhood; as it were
  An angel-watered lily, that near God
    Grows and is quiet.   Till, one dawn at home
She woke in her white bed, and had no fear
  At all,—yet wept till sunshine, and felt awed:
    Because the fulness of the time was come.

II.

THESE are the symbols.   On that cloth of red
  I' the centre is the Tripoint: perfect each,
  Except the second of its points, to teach
That Christ is not yet born.   The books—whose head
Is golden Charity, as Paul hath said—
  Those virtues are wherein the soul is rich:
  Therefore on them the lily standeth, which
Is Innocence, being interpreted.

Mary's Girlhood.

The seven-thorn'd briar and the palm seven-leaved
  Are her great sorrow and her great reward.
    Until the end be full, the Holy One
Abides without.   She soon shall have achieved
  Her perfect purity: yea, God the Lord
    Shall soon vouchsafe His Son to be her Son.

THE CARD-DEALER.

COULD you not drink her gaze like wine?
  Yet though its splendour swoon
Into the silence languidly
  As a tune into a tune,
Those eyes unravel the coiled night
  And know the stars at noon.

The gold that 's heaped beside her hand,
  In truth rich prize it were;
And rich the dreams that wreathe her brows
  With magic stillness there;
And he were rich who should unwind
  That woven golden hair.

Around her, where she sits, the dance
  Now breathes its eager heat;
And not more lightly or more true
  Fall there the dancers' feet
Than fall her cards on the bright board
  As 't were a heart that beat.

Her fingers let them softly through,
  Smooth polished silent things;
And each one as it falls reflects
  In swift light-shadowings,
Blood-red and purple, green and blue,
  The great eyes of her rings.

The Card-Dealer.

Whom plays she with? With thee, who lov'st
  Those gems upon her hand;
With me, who search her secret brows;
  With all men, bless'd or bann'd.
We play together, she and we,
  Within a vain strange land:

A land without any order,—
  Day even as night, (one saith,)—
Where who lieth down ariseth not
  Nor the sleeper awakeneth;
A land of darkness as darkness itself
  And of the shadow of death.

What be her cards, you ask? Even these:—
  The heart that doth but crave
More, having fed; the diamond,
  Skilled to make base seem brave;
The club, for smiting in the dark;
  The spade, to dig a grave.

And do you ask what game she plays?
  With me 't is lost or won;
With thee it is playing still; with him
  It is not well begun;
But 't is a game she plays with all
  Beneath the sway o' the sun.

Thou seest the card that falls,—she knows
  The card that followeth:
Her game in thy tongue is called Life,
  As ebbs thy daily breath:
When she shall speak, thou 'lt learn her tongue
  And know she calls it Death.

ON REFUSAL OF AID BETWEEN NATIONS.

THIS is one of the few political poems by Rossetti, of whose temper of mind toward public questions William Morris wrote as follows: "I can't say how it was that Rossetti took no interest in politics; but so it was: of course he was quite Italian in his general turn of thought though I think he took less interest in Italian politics than in English, in spite of his knowing several of the leading patriots personally, Saffi for instance. The truth is, he cared for nothing but individual and personal matters; chiefly of course in relation to art and literature, but he would take abundant trouble to help any one person who was in distress of mind or body; but the evils of any mass of people he could not bring his mind to bear upon." (Mackail's *William Morris,* pp. 92–93.) Rossetti himself admits to Hall Caine that he never read a Parliamentary Debate in his life, but adds that some among those whose opinions he most values think him "not altogether wrong" when he ventures to "speak of the momentary momentousness and eternal futility of many noisiest questions." The sonnet *On Refusal of Aid between Nations* refers to the apathy with which other countries witnessed the national struggles of Italy and Hungary against Austria. Before printing it in the volume of 1870 Rossetti considered giving it the somewhat elaborate title: *On the Refusal of Aid to Hungary, 1849, to Poland, 1861, to Crete, 1867.*

ON REFUSAL OF AID BETWEEN
NATIONS.

Not that the earth is changing, O my God!
  Nor that the seasons totter in their walk,—
  Not that the virulent ill of act and talk
Seethes ever as a winepress ever trod,—
Not therefore are we certain that the rod
  Weighs in thine hand to smite thy world; though now
  Beneath thine hand so many nations bow,
So many kings:—not therefore, O my God! —

But because Man is parcelled out in men
  To-day; because, for any wrongful blow
    No man not stricken asks: "I would be told
Why thou dost thus"; but his heart whispers then,
  "He is he, I am I." By this we know
    That our earth falls asunder, being old.

ON THE "VITA NUOVA" OF DANTE.

ROSSETTI began translating Dante's *Vita Nuova* when he was about seventeen years old. In his earlier youth he, together with his brother and sisters, had been alienated from study of the great Florentine by their father's absorbing interest in him and abstruse speculations concerning the interpretation to be put upon his poetry.

"Our Father, when writing about the *Commedia* or the *Vita Nuova*," says Mr. William Rossetti, "was seen surrounded by ponderous folios in italic type, 'libri mistici' and the like (often about alchemy, freemasonry, Brahminism, Swedenborg, the Cabbala, etc.), and filling page after page of prose, in impeccable handwriting, full of underscorings, interlineations, and cancellings. We contemplated his labours with a certain hushed feeling, which partook of respect and also of levity, but were assuredly not much tempted to take up one of his books, and see whether it would 'do to read.'" When Rossetti at last took up the *Vita Nuova*, however, he found it "do" so well as to inspire many of his nobler productions in painting and poetry. In his Introduction to the translation he says of it: "The *Vita Nuova* is a book which only youth could have produced, and which must chiefly remain sacred to the young; to each of whom the figure of Beatrice, less lifelike than lovelike, will seem the friend of his own heart."

ON THE "VITA NUOVA" OF DANTE.

As he that loves oft looks on the dear form
  And guesses how it grew to womanhood,
  And gladly would have watched the beauties bud
And the mild fire of precious life wax warm:
So I, long bound within the threefold charm
  Of Dante's love sublimed to heavenly mood,
  Had marvelled, touching his Beatitude,
How grew such presence from man's shameful swarm.

At length within this book I found pourtrayed
  Newborn that Paradisal Love of his,
And simple like a child; with whose clear aid
  I understood.   To such a child as this,
Christ, charging well His chosen ones, forbade
  Offence: "for lo! of such my kingdom is."

A TRIP TO PARIS AND BELGIUM.

THE trip commemorated in this group of poems was an important one for Rossetti. It was "the longest," says Mr. William Rossetti, "in point of duration and space combined, that he ever undertook." Bruges he found "a stunning place," with "a quantity of first-rate architecture, and very little or no Rubens." Here he made acquaintance with what he called "the miraculous works" of Memmling and Van Eyck. His enthusiasm for the pictures of the former was unbounded. "I assure you," he wrote home to the Brotherhood, "that the perfection of character and even drawing, the astounding finish, the glory of colour, and above all the pure religious sentiment and ecstatic poetry of these works, is not to be conceived or described." In the first version of the poem called *Antwerp and Bruges,* Memmling's name was spelled "Memmelinck," and Rossetti explains that this is "an authentic variation in the orthography of that stunner's name" and not his own invention. He adds: "The song is, of course, quite original; there is in particular a Yankee of the name of Longfellow with whose works it has no affinity." Arrived in Paris, he wrote to his brother: "The other day we walked to the Bastille. Hunt and Broodie smoked their cigars, while I, in a fine frenzy, conjured up by association and historical knowledge, leaned against the column of July and composed the following sonnet." The sonnet referred to is the one called *Place de la Bastille, Paris;* the first version of which reads as follows:

[86]

A Trip to Paris and Belgium.

How dear the sky hath been above this place !
  Small treasures of this sky that we see here,
   Seen weak through prison-bars from year to year—
Eyed with a painful prayer upon God's grace
To save, and tears which stayed along the face
  Lifted till the sun went.   How passing dear
  At night when through those bars a wind left clear
The skies and moonlight made a mournful space !
This was until, one night, the secret kept
  Safe in low vault and stealthy corridor
    Was blown abroad on a swift wind of flame
    Above, God's sky and God are still the same ;
It may be that as many tears are wept
  Beneath, and that man is but as of yore.

Antwerp and Bruges was printed in *The Germ* under the title, *The Carillon,* with *Antwerp and Bruges* for a subtitle, and a note that reads: "In these and others of the Flemish Towns, the *Carillon,* or chimes, which have a most fantastic and delicate music, are played almost continually. The custom is very ancient." In *The Germ* the poem runs as follows:

At Antwerp, there is a low wall
  Binding the city, and a moat
  Beneath, that the wind keeps afloat.
You pass the gates in a slow drawl
Of wheels. If it is warm at all
  The Carillon will give you thought.

I climed the stair in Antwerp church,
  What time the urgent weight of sound
  At sunset seems to heave it round.
Far up, the Carillon did search
The wind; and the birds came to perch
  Far under, where the gables wound.

A Trip to Paris and Belgium.

In Antwerp harbour on the Scheldt
   I stood along, a certain space
   Of night.   The mist was near my face:
Deep on, the flow was heard and felt.
The Carillon kept pause, and dwelt
   In music through the silent place.

At Bruges, when you leave the train,
   A singing numbness in your ears,—
   The Carillon's first sound appears
Only the inner moil.   Again
A little minute though — your brain
   Takes quiet, and the whole sense hears.

John Memmeling and John Van Eyck
   Hold state at Bruges.   In sore shame
   I scanned the works that keep their name.
The Carillon, which then did strike
Mine ears, was heard of theirs alike;
   It set me closer unto them.

I climed at Bruges all the flight
   The Belfry has of ancient stone.
   For leagues I saw the east wind blown:
The earth was grey, the sky was white.
I stood so near upon the height
   That my flesh felt the Carillon.

October, 1849.

A TRIP TO PARIS AND BELGIUM.

LONDON TO FOLKESTONE.

A CONSTANT keeping-past of shaken trees,
And a bewildered glitter of loose road;
Banks of bright growth, with single blades atop
Against white sky: and wires—a constant chain—
That seem to draw the clouds along with them
(Things which one stoops against the light to see
Through the low window; shaking by at rest,
Or fierce like water as the swiftness grows);
And, seen through fences or a bridge far off,
Trees that in moving keep their intervals
Still one 'twixt bar and bar; and then at times
Long reaches of green level, where one cow,
Feeding among her fellows that feed on,
Lifts her slow neck, and gazes for the sound.

Fields mown in ridges; and close garden-crops
Of the earth's increase; and a constant sky
Still with clear trees that let you see the wind;
And snatches of the engine-smoke, by fits
Tossed to the wind against the landscape, where
Rooks stooping heave their wings upon the day.

Brick walls we pass between, passed so at once
That for the suddenness I cannot know

A Trip to Paris and Belgium.

Or what, or where begun, or where at end.
Sometimes a station in grey quiet; whence,
With a short gathered champing of pent sound,
We are let out upon the air again.
Pauses of water soon, at intervals,
That has the sky in it:—the reflexes
O' the trees move towards the bank as we go by,
Leaving the water's surface plain.   I now
Lie back and close my eyes a space; for they
Smart from the open forwardness of thought
Fronting the wind.

   .   .   .   .   .   .

                 I did not scribble more,
Be certain, after this; but yawned, and read,
And nearly dozed a little, I believe;
Till, stretching up against the carriage-back,
I was roused altogether, and looked out
To where the pale sea brooded murmuring.[1]

II.

BOULOGNE TO AMIENS AND PARIS.

Strong extreme speed, that the brain hurries with,
Further than trees, and hedges, and green grass
Whitened by distance,—further than small pools
Held among fields and gardens, further than
Haystacks, and wind-mill-sails, and roofs and herds,—
The sea's last margin ceases at the sun.

The sea has left us, but the sun remains.
Sometimes the country spreads aloof in tracts
Smooth from the harvest; sometimes sky and land
Are shut from the square space the window leaves
By a dense crowd of trees, stem behind stem

A Trip to Paris and Belgium.

Passing across each other as we pass:
Sometimes tall poplar-wands stand white, their heads
Outmeasuring the distant hills.   Sometimes
The ground has a deep greenness; sometimes brown
In stubble; and sometimes no ground at all,
For the close strength of crops that stand unreaped.
The water-plots are sometimes all the sun's,—
Sometimes quite green through shadows filling them,
Or islanded with growths of reeds,—or else
Masked in grey dust like the wide face o' the fields.
And still the swiftness lasts; that to our speed
The trees seem shaken like a press of spears.

There is some count of us:—folks travelling capped,
Priesthood, and lank hard-featured soldiery,
Females (no women), blouses, Hunt, and I.

We are relayed at Amiens.   The steam
Snorts, chafes, and bridles, like three hundred horse,
And flings its dusky mane upon the air.
Our company is thinned, and lamps alight.
But still there are the folks in travelling-caps,
No priesthood now, but always soldiery,
And babies to make up for show in noise;
Females (no women), blouses, Hunt, and I.

Our windows at one side are shut for warmth;
Upon the other side, a leaden sky,
Hung in blank glare, makes all the country dim,
Which too seems bald and meagre,—be it truth,
Or of the waxing darkness.   Here and there
The shade takes light, where in thin patches stand
The unstirred dregs of water.

A Trip to Paris and Belgium.

III.

THE PARIS RAILWAY-STATION.

In France (to baffle thieves and murderers),
A journey takes two days of passport work
At least.   The plan 's sometimes a tedious one,
But bears its fruit.   Because, the other day,
In passing by the Morgue, we saw a man
(The thing is common, and we never should
Have known of it, only we passed that way)
Who had been stabbed and tumbled in the Seine,
Where he had stayed some days.   The face was black,
And, like a negro's, swollen; all the flesh
Had furred, and broken into a green mould.

Now, very likely, he who did the job
Was standing among those who stood with us,
To look upon the corpse.   You fancy him—
Smoking an early pipe, and watching, as
An artist, the effect of his last work.
This always if it had not struck him that
'T were best to leave while yet the body took
Its crust of rot beneath the Seine.   It may:
But, if it did not, he can now remain
Without much fear.   *Only,* if he should want
To travel, and have not his passport yet,
(Deep dogs these French police!) he may be caught.

Therefore you see (lest, being murderers,
We should not have the sense to go before
The thing were known, or to stay afterwards)
There is good reason why—having resolved
To start for Belgium—we were kept three days
To learn about the passports first, then do

As we had learned.   This notwithstanding, in
The fulness of the time 't is come to pass.

IV.

REACHING BRUSSELS.

There is small change of country; but the sun
Is out, and it seems shame this were not said.
For upon all the grass the warmth has caught;
And betwixt distant whitened poplar-stems
Makes greener darkness; and in dells of trees
Shows spaces of a verdure that was hid;
And the sky has its blue floated with white,
And crossed with falls of the sun's glory aslant
To lay upon the waters of the world;
And from the road men stand with shaded eyes
To look; and flowers in gardens have grown strong;
And our own shadows here within the coach
Are brighter; and all colour has more bloom.

So, after the sore torments of the route;—
Toothache, and headache, and the ache of wind,
And huddled sleep, and smarting wakefulness,
And night, and day, and hunger sick at food,
And twenty-fold relays, and packages
To be unlocked, and passports to be found,
And heavy well-kept landscape;—we were glad
Because we entered Brussels in the sun.

V.

ANTWERP TO GHENT.

We are upon the Scheldt.   We know we move
Because there is a floating at our eyes

A Trip to Paris and Belgium.

Whatso they seek; and because all the things
Which on our outset were distinct and large
Are smaller and much weaker and quite grey,
And at last gone from us.   No motion else.

   We are upon the road.   The thin swift moon
Runs with the running clouds that are the sky,
And with the running water runs — at whiles
Weak 'neath the film and heavy growth of reeds.
The country swims with motion.   Time itself
Is consciously beside us, and perceived.
Our speed is such the sparks our engine leaves
Are burning after the whole train has passed.

The darkness is a tumult.   We tear on,
The roll behind us and the cry before,
Constantly, in a lull of intense speed
And thunder.   Any other sound is known
Merely by sight.   The shrubs, the trees your eye
Scans for their growth, are far along in haze.
The sky has lost its clouds, and lies away
Oppressively at calm: the moon has failed:
Our speed has set the wind against us.   Now
Our engine's heat is fiercer, and flings up
Great glares alongside.   Wind and steam and speed
And clamour and the night.   We are in Ghent.

THE STAIRCASE OF NOTRE DAME, PARIS.

As one who, groping in a narrow stair,
  Hath a strong sound of bells upon his ears,
  Which, being at a distance off, appears
Quite close to him because of the pent air:
So with this France. She stumbles file and square
  Darkling and without space for breath: each one
  Who hears the thunder says: "It shall anon
Be in among her ranks to scatter her."

This may be; and it may be that the storm
  Is spent in rain upon the unscathed seas,
    Or wasteth other countries ere it die:
Till she,—having climbed always through the swarm
  Of darkness and of hurtling sound,—from these
    Shall step forth on the light in a still sky.

PLACE DE LA BASTILLE, PARIS.

How dear the sky has been above this place!
  Small treasures of this sky that we see here
  Seen weak through prison-bars from year to year;
Eyed with a painful prayer upon God's grace
To save, and tears that stayed along the face
  Lifted at sunset. Yea, how passing dear,
  Those nights when through the bars a wind left clear
The heaven, and moonlight soothed the limpid space!

So was it, till one night the secret kept
  Safe in low vault and stealthy corridor
    Was blown abroad on gospel-tongues of flame.
  O ways of God, mysterious evermore!
How many on this spot have cursed and wept
    That all might stand here now and own Thy Name.

NEAR BRUSSELS — A HALF-WAY PAUSE.

THE turn of noontide has begun.
   In the weak breeze the sunshine yields.
   There is a bell upon the fields.
On the long hedgerow's tangled run
   A low white cottage intervenes:
   Against the wall a blind man leans,
And sways his face to have the sun.

Our horses' hoofs stir in the road,
   Quiet and sharp.   Light hath a song
   Whose silence, being heard, seems long.
The point of noon maketh abode,
   And will not be at once gone through.
   The sky's deep colour saddens you,
And the heat weighs a dreamy load.

ANTWERP AND BRUGES.

I CLIMBED the stair in Antwerp church,
   What time the circling thews of sound
   At sunset seem to heave it round.
Far up, the carillon did search
The wind, and the birds came to perch
   Far under, where the gables wound.   .

In Antwerp harbour on the Scheldt
   I stood along, a certain space
   Of night.   The mist was near my face;
Deep on, the flow was heard and felt.
The carillon kept pause, and dwelt
   In music through the silent place.

John Memmeling and John van Eyck
   Hold state at Bruges.   In sore shame
   I scanned the works that keep their name.
The carillon, which then did strike
Mine ears, was heard of theirs alike:
   It set me closer unto them.

I climbed at Bruges all the flight
   The belfry has of ancient stone.
   For leagues I saw the east wind blown;
The earth was grey, the sky was white.
I stood so near upon the height
   That my flesh felt the carillon.

ON LEAVING BRUGES.

THE city's steeple-towers remove away,
   Each singly; as each vain infatuate Faith
   Leaves God in heaven, and passes. A mere breath
Each soon appears, so far. Yet that which lay
The first is now scarce further or more grey
   Than the last is. Now all are wholly gone.
   The sunless sky has not once had the sun
Since the first weak beginning of the day.

The air falls back as the wind finishes,
   And the clouds stagnate. On the water's face
      The current breathes along, but is not stirred.
      There is no branch that thrills with any bird.
   Winter is to possess the earth a space,
And have its will upon the extreme seas.

FOR A VIRGIN AND CHILD.

BY HANS MEMMELINCK.

(In the Academy of Bruges.)

MYSTERY: God, man's life, born into man
  Of woman.   There abideth on her brow
  The ended pang of knowledge, the which now
Is calm assured.   Since first her task began
She hath known all.   What more of anguish than
  Endurance oft hath lived through, the whole space
  Through night till day, passed weak upon her face
While the heard lapse of darkness slowly ran ?[1]

All hath been told her touching her dear Son,
  And all shall be accomplished.   Where He sits
    Even now, a babe, He holds the symbol fruit
  Perfect and chosen.   Until God permits,
    His soul's elect still have the absolute
Harsh nether darkness, and make painful moan.

The Boat of Love.

Unfinished picture, 1874

FOR A MARRIAGE OF ST. CATHERINE.

IN *The Germ* the octave of this sonnet reads as
follows:

> MYSTERY: Katharine, the bride of Christ.
> She kneels, and on her hand the holy Child
> Setteth the ring.   Her life is sad and mild,
> Laid in God's knowledge—ever unenticed
> From Him, and in the end thus fitly priced.
> Awe, and the music that is near her, wrought
> Of Angels, hath possessed her eyes in thought:
> Her utter joy is her's, and hath sufficed.

FOR A MARRIAGE OF ST. CATHERINE.

BY HANS MEMMELINCK.

(In the Hospital of St. John at Bruges.)

MYSTERY: Catherine the bride of Christ.
  She kneels, and on her hand the holy Child
  Now sets the ring.   Her life is hushed and mild,
Laid in God's knowledge — ever unenticed
From God, and in the end thus fitly priced.
  Awe, and the music that is near her, wrought
  Of angels, have possessed her eyes in thought:
Her utter joy is hers, and hath sufficed.

There is a pause while Mary Virgin turns
  The leaf, and reads.   With eyes on the spread book,
    That damsel at her knees reads after her.
    John whom He loved, and John His harbinger,
  Listen and watch.   Whereon soe'er thou look,
The light is starred in gems and the gold burns.

FOR AN ALLEGORICAL DANCE OF WOMEN.

BY ANDREA MANTEGNA.

THIS sonnet as it appeared in *The Germ* read as
follows:

A DANCE OF NYMPHS.

BY ANDREA MANTEGNA.

(In the Louvre.)

(**** It is necessary to mention that this picture would
appear to have been in the artist's mind an allegory,
which the modern spectator may seek vainly to interpret.)

Scarcely, I think; yet it indeed *may* be
   The meaning reached him, when this music rang
   Sharp through his brain, a distinct rapid pang,
And he beheld these rocks and that ridg'd sea
But I believe he just leaned passively,
   And felt their hair carried across his face
   As each nymph passed him; nor gave ear to trace
How many feet; nor bent assuredly
His eyes from the blind fixedness of thought
   To see the dancers.   It is bitter glad
    Even unto tears.   Its meaning filleth it,
    A portion of most secret life: to wit:—
   Each human pulse shall keep the sense it had
With all, though the mind's labour run to nought.

FOR AN ALLEGORICAL DANCE OF WOMEN.

BY ANDREA MANTEGNA.

(In the Louvre.)

SCARCELY, I think; yet it indeed *may* be
 The meaning reached him, when this music rang
 Clear through his frame, a sweet possessive pang,
And he beheld these rocks and that ridged sea.
But I believe that, leaning tow'rds them, he
 Just felt their hair carried across his face
 As each girl passed him; nor gave ear to trace
How many feet; nor bent assuredly
His eyes from the blind fixedness of thought
 To know the dancers.   It is bitter glad
  Even unto tears.   Its meaning filleth it,
  A secret of the wells of Life: to wit:—
 The heart's each pulse shall keep the sense it had
With all, though the mind's labour run to nought.

FOR A VENETIAN PASTORAL.

T HIS sonnet appeared in *The Germ* with the follow-
ing note:

" In this picture, two cavaliers and an undraped wo-
man are seated in the grass, with musical instruments,
while another woman dips a vase into a well hard by,
for water."

The Germ version of the Sonnet reads:

Water, for anguish of the solstice,—yea,
   Over the vessel's mouth still widening
   Listlessly dipt to let the water in
With slow vague gurgle.   Blue, and deep away,
The heat lies silent at the brink of day.
   Now the hand trails upon the viol-string
   That sobs; and the brown faces cease to sing,
Mournful with complete pleasure.   Her eyes stray
In distance; through her lips the pipe doth creep
   And leaves them pouting; the green shadowed grass
   Is cool against her naked flesh.   Let be:
Do not now speak unto her lest she weep,—
   Nor name this ever.   Be it as it was:—
   Silence of heat and solemn poetry.

FOR A VENETIAN PASTORAL.

BY GIORGIONE.

(In the Louvre.)

WATER, for anguish of the solstice:—nay,
  But dip the vessel slowly,—nay, but lean
  And hark how at its verge the wave sighs in
Reluctant. Hush! beyond all depth away
The heat lies silent at the brink of day:
  Now the hand trails upon the viol-string
  That sobs, and the brown faces cease to sing,
Sad with the whole of pleasure. Whither stray
Her eyes now, from whose mouth the slim pipes creep
  And leave it pouting, while the shadowed grass
    Is cool against her naked side? Let be:—
Say nothing now unto her lest she weep,
  Nor name this ever. Be it as it was,—
    Life touching lips with Immortality.

The first form of these sonnets is given in the *Family Letters of Dante Gabriel Rossetti* as follows:

LAST VISIT TO THE LUXEMBOURG.
ROGER RESCUING ANGELICA; BY INGRES.

I.

A ʀᴇᴍᴏᴛᴇ sky, that meeteth the sea's brim;
   One rock-point standing buffeted alone,
   Vexed at its base with a foul beast unknown,
Hell-spurge of geomaunt and teraphim:
A knight, and a winged creature bearing him,
   Reared at the rock: a woman fettered there,
   Leaning into the hollow with loose hair
And throat let back and heartsick trail of limb.
The sky is harsh, and the sea shrewd and salt.
   Under his lord the griffin-horse ramps blind
      With rigid wings and tail.   The spear's lithe stem
   Stands in the roaring of those jaws; behind,
The evil length of body chafes at halt.
      She doth not hear or see—she knows of them.

II.

Clench thine eyes now,—'t is the last instant, girl:
   Draw in thy senses, loose thy knees, and shake:
   Set thy breath fast: thy life is keen awake,—
Thou mayst not swoon.   Was that the scattered whirl
Of its foam drenched thee? or the waves that curl
   And split—bleak spray wherein thy temples ache?
   Or was it his thy champion's blood, to flake
That flesh which has the colour of fine pearl?
Now silence: for the sea's is such a sound
   As irks not silence, and except the sea
      All is now still.   Now the dead thing doth cease
   To writhe and drifts.   He turns to her; and she,
Cast from the jaws of Death, remains there bound,
      Again a woman in her nakedness.

[107]

FOR
RUGGIERO AND ANGELICA.[1]

BY INGRES.

(1849.)

:.

A REMOTE sky, prolonged to the sea's brim:
　　One rock-point standing buffeted alone,
　　Vexed at its base with a foul beast unknown,
Hell-birth of geomaunt and teraphim:
A knight, and a winged creature bearing him,
　　Reared at the rock: a woman fettered there,
　　Leaning into the hollow with loose hair
And throat let back and heartsick trail of limb.

The sky is harsh, and the sea shrewd and salt:
　　Under his lord the griffin-horse ramps blind
　　　With rigid wings and tail.　The spear's lithe stem
Thrills in the roaring of those jaws: behind,
That evil length of body chafes at fault.
　　She does not hear nor see—she knows of them.

II.

Clench thine eyes now,—'t is the last instant, girl :
　　Draw in thy senses, set thy knees, and take
　　One breath for all: thy life is keen awake,—
Thou mayst not swoon.　Was that the scattered whirl
Of its foam drenched thee ?—or the waves that curl

For Ruggiero and Angelica.

And split, bleak spray wherein thy temples ache?
Or was it his the champion's blood to flake
Thy flesh?—or thine own blood's anointing, girl?

Now, silence: for the sea's is such a sound
  As irks not silence; and except the sea,
    All now is still. Now the dead thing doth cease
  To writhe, and drifts. He turns to her: and she,
Cast from the jaws of Death, remains there, bound,
    Again a woman in her nakedness.

FOR
AN ANNUNCIATION.

EARLY GERMAN.

THE lilies stand before her like a screen
   Through which, upon this warm and solemn day,
   God surely hears.   For there she kneels to pray
Who wafts our prayers to God—Mary the Queen.
She was Faith's Present, parting what had been
   From what began with her, and is for aye.
   On either hand, God's twofold system lay:
With meek bowed face a Virgin prayed between.

So prays she, and the Dove flies in to her,
   And she has turned.   At the low porch is one
     Who looks as though deep awe made him to smile.
Heavy with heat, the plants yield shadow there;
   The loud flies cross each other in the sun;
     And the aisled pillars meet the poplar-aisle.

FOR
OUR LADY OF THE ROCKS.

BY LEONARDO DA VINCI.

MOTHER, is this the darkness of the end,
   The Shadow of Death ? and is that outer sea
   Infinite imminent Eternity ?
And does the death-pang by man's seed sustained
In Time's each instant cause thy face to bend
   Its silent prayer upon the Son, while He
   Blesses the dead with His hand silently
To His long day which hours no more offend ?

Mother of grace, the pass is difficult,
   Keen as these rocks, and the bewildered souls
     Throng it like echoes, blindly shuddering through.
   Thy name, O Lord, each spirit's voice extols,
     Whose peace abides in the dark avenue
Amid the bitterness of things occult.

AVE.

THIS, with certain other early poems of religious tone, Rossetti at one time grouped under the title *Songs of the Art Catholic*, by which he meant to suggest, Mr. William Rossetti thinks, that the poems "embodied conceptions and a point of view related to pictorial art — also that this art was in sentiment, though not necessarily in dogma, Catholic — mediæval and un-modern." Of the dogmatic suggestion in *Ave* Rossetti was somewhat afraid when he revived the poem for his volume of 1870. "I hesitated much to print *Ave*," he wrote to his brother, "because of the subject; but thought it well done, and so included it."

The Salutation of Beatrice : The Meeting in Florence.   (1859.)

AVE.*

MOTHER of the Fair Delight,
Thou handmaid perfect in God's sight,
Now sitting fourth beside the Three,
Thyself a woman-Trinity, —
Being a daughter born to God,
Mother of Christ from stall to rood,
And wife unto the Holy Ghost: —
Oh when our need is uttermost,
Think that to such as death may strike
Thou once wert sister sisterlike!
Thou headstone of humanity,
Groundstone of the great Mystery,
Fashioned like us, yet more than we!

Mind'st thou not (when June's heavy breath
Warmed the long days in Nazareth)
That eve thou didst go forth to give
Thy flowers some drink that they might live
One faint night more amid the sands?
Far off the trees were as pale wands
Against the fervid sky: the sea
Sighed further off eternally
As human sorrow sighs in sleep.
Then suddenly the awe grew deep,
As of a day to which all days
Were footsteps in God's secret ways:

* A church legend of the Blessed Virgin's death.

Ave.

Until a folding sense, like prayer,
Which is, as God is, everywhere,
Gathered about thee; and a voice
Spake to thee without any noise,
Being of the silence: — "Hail," it said,
"Thou that art highly favourèd;
The Lord is with thee here and now;
Blessed among all women thou."

   Ah! knew'st thou of the end, when first
That Babe was on thy bosom nurs'd? —
Or when He tottered round thy knee
Did thy great sorrow dawn on thee? —
And through His boyhood, year by year
Eating with Him the Passover,
Didst thou discern confusedly
That holier sacrament, when He,
The bitter cup about to quaff,
Should break the bread and eat thereof? —
Or came not yet the knowledge, even
Till on some day forecast in Heaven
His feet passed through thy door to press
Upon His Father's business? —
Or still was God's high secret kept?

   Nay, but I think the whisper crept
Like growth through childhood. Work and play,
Things common to the course of day,
Awed thee with meanings unfulfill'd;
And all through girlhood, something still'd
Thy senses like the birth of light,
When thou hast trimmed thy lamp at night
Or washed thy garments in the stream;
To whose white bed had come the dream

Ave.

That He was thine and thou wast His
Who feeds among the field-lilies.
O solemn shadow of the end
In that wise spirit long contain'd!
O awful end! and those unsaid
Long years when It was Finishèd!

Mind'st thou not (when the twilight gone
Left darkness in the house of John,)
Between the naked window-bars
That spacious vigil of the stars?—
For thou, a watcher even as they,
Wouldst rise from where throughout the day
Thou wroughtest raiment for His poor;
And, finding the fixed terms endure
Of day and night which never brought
Sounds of His coming chariot,
Wouldst lift through cloud-waste unexplor'd
Those eyes which said, "How long, O Lord?"
Then that disciple whom He loved,
Well heeding, haply would be moved
To ask thy blessing in His name;
And that one thought in both, the same
Though silent, then would clasp ye round
To weep together,— tears long bound,
Sick tears of patience, dumb and slow.
Yet, "Surely I come quickly,"— so
He said, from life and death gone home.
Amen: even so, Lord Jesus, come!

But oh! what human tongue can speak
That day when Michael came to break[1]
From the tir'd spirit, like a veil,
Its covenant with Gabriel

Ave.

Endured at length unto the end?
What human thought can apprehend
That mystery of motherhood
When thy Beloved at length renew'd
The sweet communion severèd,—
His left hand underneath thine head
And His right hand embracing thee?—
Lo! He was thine, and this is He!

Soul, is it Faith, or Love, or Hope,
That lets me see her standing up
Where the light of the Throne is bright?
Unto the left, unto the right,
The cherubim, succinct, conjoint,
Float inward to a golden point,
And from between the seraphim
The glory issues for a hymn.
O Mary Mother, be not loth
To listen,—thou whom the stars clothe,
Who seèst and mayst not be seen!
Hear us at last, O Mary Queen!
Into our shadow bend thy face,
Bowing thee from the secret place,
O Mary Virgin, full of grace!

WORLD'S WORTH.

A CRITIC writing for *The Catholic World* concerning what he calls "Rossetti's essentially Catholic tone," says of this poem: "It is not unlike a thought from Thomas à Kempis elaborated into verse. That it should have been written by the son of a Neapolitan revolutionist and exile, who with his wife had lost the faith, and by a man who never outwardly professed a belief in Catholicity, would seem to mean that Rossetti inherited from more faithful ancestors a kind of sentiment which neither home influence nor education in acknowledged religious beliefs could have produced."

Although Rossetti became a sceptic very early in his life he was certainly not the generally accepted type of atheist. "Although he had been trained in the Anglican Church," writes his brother, "such Christian sympathies as he had went entirely in the direction of Catholicism, and not in the least of Protestantism." And from the same authority we learn that he had "an abiding and very deep reverence for the person of Christ"; holding Him to be "certainly something more than man."

In *The Germ* the following poem was printed under the title *Pax Vobis* and ran thus :

> 'T is of the Father Hilary.
>> He strove, but could not pray: so took
>> The darkened stair, where his feet shook
>> A sad blind echo. He kept up

World's Worth.

Slowly.   'T was a chill sway of air
  That autumn noon within the stair,
Sick, dizzy, like a turning cup.
  His brain perplexed him, void and thin :
  He shut his eyes and felt it spin ;
  The obscure deafness hemmed him in.
He said : " The air is calm outside."

He leaned unto the gallery
  Where the chime keeps the night and day :
  It hurt his brain,—he could not pray.
He had his face upon the stone ;
  Deep 'twixt the narrow shafts, his eye
  Passed all the roofs unto the sky
Whose greyness the wind swept alone.
  Close by his feet he saw it shake
  With wind in pools that the rains make ;
  The ripple set his eyes to ache.
He said : " Calm hath its peace outside."

He stood within the mystery
  Girding God's blessed Eucharist :
  The organ and the chaunt had ceased :
A few words paused against his ear,
  Said from the altar : drawn round him,
  The silence was at rest and dim.
He could not pray.   The bell shook clear
  And ceased.   All was great awe,—the breath
  Of God in man, that warranteth
  Wholly the inner things of Faith.
He said : " There is the world outside."

Ghent: Church of St. Bavon.

WORLD'S WORTH.

'T is of the Father Hilary.
  He strove, but could not pray; so took
  The steep-coiled stair, where his feet shook
A sad blind echo.   Ever up
  He toiled.   'T was a sick sway of air
  That autumn noon within the stair,
As dizzy as a turning cup.
  His brain benumbed him, void and thin;
  He shut his eyes and felt it spin;
  The obscure deafness hemmed him in.
He said: "O world, what world for me?"

He leaned unto the balcony
  Where the chime keeps the night and day;
  It hurt his brain, he could not pray.
He had his face upon the stone:
  Deep 'twixt the narrow shafts, his eye
  Passed all the roofs to the stark sky,
Swept with no wing, with wind alone.
  Close to his feet the sky did shake
  With wind in pools that the rains make:
  The ripples set his eyes to ache.
He said: "O world, what world for me?"

He stood within the mystery
  Girding God's blessed Eucharist:
  The organ and the chaunt had ceas'd.

World's Worth.

The last words paused against his ear
   Said from the altar: drawn round him
   The gathering rest was dumb and dim.
And now the sacring-bell rang clear
   And ceased; and all was awe,—the breath
   Of God in man that warranteth
   The inmost, utmost things of faith.
He said: "O God, my world in Thee!"

SONG AND MUSIC.

O LEAVE your hand where it lies cool
   Upon the eyes whose lids are hot:
Its rosy shade is bountiful
   Of silence, and assuages thought.
O lay your lips against your hand
   And let me feel your breath through it,
While through the sense your song shall fit
    The soul to understand.

The music lives upon my brain
   Between your hands within mine eyes;
It stirs your lifted throat like pain,
   An aching pulse of melodies.
Lean nearer, let the music pause:
   The soul may better understand
Your music, shadowed in your hand
    Now while the song withdraws.

THE SEA-LIMITS.

THE germ of this beautiful lyric is found in a couple of stanzas written on Rossetti's foreign trip of 1849. These were entitled, "At Boulogne. Upon the Cliffs: Noon," and ran as follows:

> The Sea is in its listless chime,
>   Like Time's lapse rendered audible;
>   The murmur of the earth's large shell.
> In a sad blueness beyond rhyme
>   It ends; Sense, without Thought, can pass
>   No stadium further. Since Time was,
> This sound hath told the lapse of Time.
>
> No stagnance that Death wins,—it hath
>   The mournfulness of ancient Life,
>   Always enduring at dull strife
> Like the world's heart, in calm and wrath
>   Its painful pulse is in the sands.
>   Last utterly, the whole sky stands,
> Grey and not known, along its path.

As it was printed in *The Germ* the second line of the first stanza read: "Time's lapse it is, made audible,"—and the fourth line of the second stanza read: "As the world's heart of rest and wrath." The title in *The Germ* was "From the Cliffs: Noon."

THE SEA-LIMITS.

(1849–55.)

CONSIDER the sea's listless chime:
  Time's self it is, made audible,—
  The murmur of the earth's own shell.
Secret continuance sublime
  Is the sea's end: our sight may pass
  No furlong further.   Since time was,
This sound hath told the lapse of time.

No quiet, which is death's,—it hath
  The mournfulness of ancient life,
  Enduring always at dull strife.
As the world's heart of rest and wrath,
  Its painful pulse is in the sands.
  Last utterly, the whole sky stands,
Grey and not known, along its path.

Listen alone beside the sea,
  Listen alone among the woods;
  Those voices of twin solitudes
Shall have one sound alike to thee:
  Hark where the murmurs of thronged men
  Surge and sink back and surge again,—
Still the one voice of wave and tree.

Gather a shell from the strown beach
  And listen at its lips: they sigh
  The same desire and mystery,
The echo of the whole sea's speech.
  And all mankind is thus at heart
  Not anything but what thou art:
And Earth, Sea, Man, are all in each.

VOX ECCLESIÆ, VOX CHRISTI.

(1849.)

I saw under the altar the souls of them that were slain for the word of God, and for the testimony which they held; and they cried with a loud voice, saying, How long, O Lord, holy and true, dost Thou not judge and avenge our blood on them that dwell on the earth ? — Rev. vi. 9, 10.

Not 'neath the altar only,—yet, in sooth,
   There more than elsewhere,—is the cry, "How long?"
   The right sown there hath still borne fruit in wrong—
The wrong waxed fourfold.   Thence, (in hate of truth)
O'er weapons blessed for carnage, to fierce youth
   From evil age, the word hath hissed along:—
   "Ye are the Lord's: go forth, destroy, be strong:
Christ's Church absolves ye from Christ's law of ruth."

Therefore the wine-cup at the altar is
   As Christ's own blood indeed, and as the blood
     Of Christ's elect, at divers seasons spilt
On the altar-stone, that to man's church, for this,
   Shall prove a stone of stumbling,—whence it stood
     To be rent up ere the true Church be built.

DANTE AT VERONA.

THIS poem, originally called *Dante in Exile,* was written as an introduction to Rossetti's translation of Dante's *Vita Nuova,* and is filled with allusions to the facts of Dante's career presupposing a considerable familiarity with that career on the part of the reader.

Rossetti's inheritance of Italian sympathies, not commonly obvious in his expression of himself, is here revealed with striking effect. None but an Italian could so intimately have rendered the mood of an Italian despised and rejected by his city, and sentenced to permanent exile for his passionate labours on her behalf :

> Arriving only to depart,
> From court to court, from land to land,
> Like flame within the naked hand
> His body bore his burning heart.

The picture of the great Ghibelline, angry and embittered with his fate, yet mild with the girls about the fountain, murmuring to them concerning Beatrice, is a picture no Englishman could have drawn, and no Englishman could so have depicted the quivering sensitiveness of Dante's temper without suggesting effeminacy. In *Dante at Verona,* Rossetti's subject called forth the latent force and gravity of his own nature so compellingly as to place this poem of his boyhood above most of his later poetry in beauty of thought and diction if not in regularity of form.

During what is called the "first periods" of Rossetti's

*. . S. . . . . (R. . . : The Meeting
in Paradise. (1859.)*

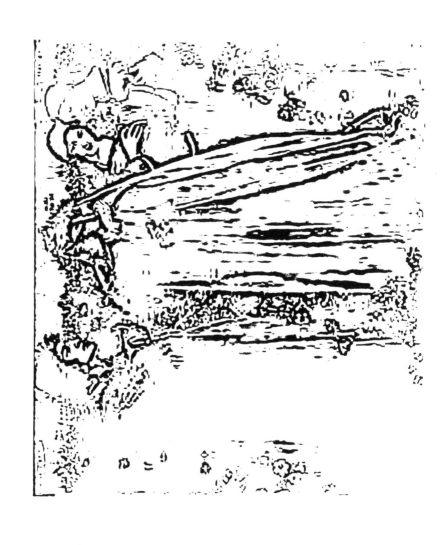

Dante at Verona.

Therefore, the loftier rose the song
  To touch the secret things of God,
  The deeper pierced the hate that trod
On base men's track who wrought the wrong;
  Till the soul's effluence came to be
  Its own exceeding agony.

Arriving only to depart,
  From court to court, from land to land,
  Like flame within the naked hand
His body bore his burning heart
  That still on Florence strove to bring
  God's fire for a burnt offering.

Even such was Dante's mood, when now,
  Mocked for long years with Fortune's sport
  He dwelt at yet another court,
There where Verona's knee did bow
  And her voice hailed with all acclaim
  Can Grande della Scala's name.

As that lord's kingly guest awhile
  His life we follow; through the days
  Which walked in exile's barren ways,—
The nights which still beneath one smile
  Heard through all spheres one song increase,—
  " Even I, even I am Beatrice."

At Can La Scala's court, no doubt,
  Due reverence did his steps attend;
  The ushers on his path would bend
At ingoing as at going out;
  The penmen waited on his call
  At council-board, the grooms in hall.

Dante at Verona.

And pages hushed their laughter down,
   And gay squires stilled the merry stir,
   When he passed up the dais-chamber
With set brows lordlier than a frown;
   And tire-maids hidden among these
   Drew close their loosened bodices.

Perhaps the priests, (exact to span
   All God's circumference,) if at whiles
   They found him wandering in their aisles,
Grudged ghostly greeting to the man
   By whom, though not of ghostly guild,
   With Heaven and Hell men's hearts were fill'd.

And the court-poets (he, forsooth,
   A whole world's poet strayed to court!)
   Had for his scorn their hate's retort.
He 'd meet them flushed with easy youth,
   Hot on their errands.   Like noon-flies
   They vexed him in the ears and eyes.

But at this court, peace still must wrench
   Her chaplet from the teeth of war:
   By day they held high watch afar,
At night they cried across the trench;
   And still, in Dante's path, the fierce
   Gaunt soldiers wrangled o'er their spears.

But vain seemed all the strength to him,
   As golden convoys sunk at sea
   Whose wealth might root out penury:
Because it was not, limb with limb,
   Knit like his heart-strings round the wall
   Of Florence, that ill pride might fall.

The first Anniversary of the Death of Beatrice: Dante drawing the angel.

pen and ink 1849

Dante at Verona.

Yet in the tiltyard, when the dust
   Cleared from the sundered press of knights
   Ere yet again it swoops and smites,
He almost deemed his longing must
   Find force to wield that multitude
   And hurl that strength the way he would.

How should he move them,—fame and gain
   On all hands calling them at strife?
   He still might find but his one life
To give, by Florence counted vain:
   One heart the false hearts made her doubt,
   One voice she heard once and cast out.

Oh! if his Florence could but come,
   A lily-sceptred damsel fair,
   As her own Giotto painted her
On many shields and gates at home,—
   A lady crowned, at a soft pace
   Riding the lists round to the dais:

Till where Can Grande rules the lists,
   As young as Truth, as calm as Force,
   She draws her rein now, while her horse
Bows at the turn of the white wrists;
   And when each knight within his stall
   Gives ear, she speaks and tells them all:

All the foul tale,—truth sworn untrue
   And falsehood's triumph.   All the tale?
   Great God! and must she not prevail
To fire them ere they heard it through,—
   And hand achieve ere heart could rest
   That high adventure of her quest?

Dante at Verona.

The window thou, a youth, hast sought,
  Flushed in the limpid eventime,
  Ending with daylight the day's rhyme
Of her; where oftenwhiles her thought
  Held thee—the lamp untrimmed to write—
  In joy through the blue lapse of night.

At Can La Scala's court, no doubt,
  Guests seldom wept. It was brave sport,
  No doubt, at Can La Scala's court,
Within the palace and without;
  Where music, set to madrigals,
  Loitered all day through groves and halls.

Because Can Grande of his life
  Had not had six-and-twenty years
  As yet. And when the chroniclers
Tell you of that Vicenza strife
  And of strifes elsewhere,—you must not
  Conceive for church-sooth he had got

Just nothing in his wits but war:
  Though doubtless 't was the young man's joy
  (Grown with his growth from a mere boy,)
To mark his "Viva Cane!" scare
  The foe's shut front, till it would reel
  All blind with shaken points of steel.

But there were places—held too sweet
  For eyes that had not the due veil
  Of lashes and clear lids—as well
In favour as his saddle-seat:
  Breath of low speech he scorned not there
  Nor light cool fingers in his hair.

Dante at Verona.

Yet if the child whom the sire's plan
  Made free of a deep treasure-chest
  Scoffed it with ill-conditioned jest,—
We may be sure too that the man
  Was not mere thews, nor all content
  With lewdness swathed in sentiment.

So you may read and marvel not
  That such a man as Dante—one
  Who, while Can Grande's deeds were done,
Had drawn his robe round him and thought—
  Now at the same guest-table far'd
  Where keen Uguccio wiped his beard.[1]

Through leaves and trellis-work the sun
  Left the wine cool within the glass,—
  They feasting where no sun could pass:
And when the women, all as one,
  Rose up with brightened cheeks to go,
  It was a comely thing, we know.

But Dante recked not of the wine;
  Whether the women stayed or went,
  His visage held one stern intent:
And when the music had its sign
  To breathe upon them for more ease,
  Sometimes he turned and bade it cease.

And as he spared not to rebuke
  The mirth, so oft in council he
  To bitter truth bore testimony:
And when the crafty balance shook
  Well poised to make the wrong prevail,
  Then Dante's hand would turn the scale.

Figure of Dante from " Dante's Dream," 1871. ... as:

!mb.

wealth

Dante at Verona.

Then, facing on his guest, he cried,—
  "Say, Messer Dante, how it is
  I get out of a clown like this
More than your wisdom can provide."
  And Dante: "'T is man's ancient whim
  That still his like seems good to him."

Also a tale is told, how once,
  At clearing tables after meat,
  Piled for a jest at Dante's feet
Were found the dinner's well-picked bones;
  So laid, to please the banquet's lord,
  By one who crouched beneath the board.

Then smiled Can Grande to the rest:
  "Our Dante's tuneful mouth indeed
  Lacks not the gift on flesh to feed!"
"Fair host of mine," replied the guest,
  "So many bones you'd not descry
  If so it chanced the *dog* were I."[3]

But wherefore should we turn the grout
  In a drained cup, or be at strife
  From the worn garment of a life
To rip the twisted ravel out?
  Good needs expounding; but of ill
  Each hath enough to guess his fill.

They named him Justicer-at-Law:
  Each month to bear the tale in mind
  Of hues a wench might wear unfin'd
And of the load an ox might draw;
  To cavil in the weight of bread
  And to see purse-thieves gibbeted.

Dante at Verona.

And when his spirit wove the spell
  (From under even to over-noon
  In converse with itself alone,)
As high as Heaven, as low as Hell,—
  He would be summoned and must go:
  For had not Gian stabbed Giacomo?

Therefore the bread he had to eat
  Seemed brackish, less like corn than tares;
  And the rush-strown, accustomed stairs
Each day were steeper to his feet;
  And when the night-vigil was done,
  His brows would ache to feel the sun.

Nevertheless, when from his kin
  There came the tidings how at last
  In Florence a decree was pass'd
Whereby all banish'd folk might win
  Free pardon, so a fine were paid
  And act of public penance made,—

This Dante writ in answer thus,
  Words such as these: "That clearly they
  In Florence must not have to say,—
The man abode aloof from us
  Nigh fifteen years, yet lastly skulk'd
  Hither to candleshrift and mulct.

"That he was one the Heavens forbid
  To traffic in God's justice sold
  By market-weight of earthly gold,
Or to bow down over the lid
  Of steaming censers, and so be
  Made clean of manhood's obloquy.

Dante at Verona.

"That since 'no gate led, by God's will,
   To Florence, but the one whereat
   The priests and money-changers sat,
He still would wander; for that still,
   Even through the body's prison-bars,
   His soul possessed the sun and stars."

Such were his words.   It is indeed
   For ever well our singers should
   Utter good words and know them good
Not through song only; with close heed
   Lest, having spent for the work's sake
   Six days, the man be left to make.

Months o'er Verona, till the feast
   Was come for Florence the Free Town:
   And at the shrine of Baptist John
The exiles, girt with many a priest
   And carrying candles as they went,
   Were held to mercy of the saint.

On the high seats in sober state,—
   Gold neck-chains range o'er range below
   Gold screen-work where the lilies grow,—
The heads of the Republic sate,
   Marking the humbled face go by
   Each one of his house-enemy.

And as each proscript rose and stood
   From kneeling in the ashen dust
   On the shrine-steps, some magnate thrust
A beard into the velvet hood
   Of his front colleague's gown, to see
   The cinders stuck in his bare knee.

Dante at Verona.

The trust which he had borne in youth
  Was all at length accomplished. He
  At length had written worthily—
Yea even of her; no rhymes uncouth
  'Twixt tongue and tongue; but by God's aid
  The first words Italy had said.

Ah! haply now the heavenly guide
  Was not the last form seen by him:
  But there that Beatrice stood slim
And bowed in passing at his side,
  For whom in youth his heart made moan
  Then when the city sat alone. •

Clearly herself: the same whom he
  Met, not past girlhood, in the street,
  Low-bosomed and with hidden feet;
And then as woman perfectly,
  In years that followed, many an once,—
  And now at last among the suns

In that high vision. But indeed
  It may be memory might recall
  Last to him then the first of all,—
The child his boyhood bore in heed
  Nine years. At length the voice brought peace,—
  "Even I, even I am Beatrice."

All this, being there, we had not seen.
  Seen only was the shadow wrought
  On the strong features bound in thought;
The vagueness gaining gait and mien;
  The white streaks gathering clear to view
  In the burnt beard the women knew.

Dante at Verona.

For a tale tells that on his track,
  As through Verona's streets he went,
  This saying certain women sent:—
"Lo, he that strolls to Hell and back
  At will!   Behold him, how Hell's reek
  Has crisped his beard and singed his cheek."

"Whereat" (Boccaccio's words) "he smil'd
  For pride in fame."   It might be so:
  Nevertheless we cannot know
If haply he were not beguil'd
  To bitterer mirth, who scarce could tell
  If he indeed were back from Hell.

So the day came, after a space,
  When Dante felt assured that there
  The sunshine must lie sicklier
Even than in any other place,
  Save only Florence.   When that day
  Had come, he rose and went his way.

He went and turned not.   From his shoes
  It may be that he shook the dust,
  As every righteous dealer must
Once and again ere life can close:
  And unaccomplished destiny
  Struck cold his forehead, it may be.

No book keeps record how the Prince
  Sunned himself out of Dante's reach,
  Nor how the Jester stank in speech:
While courtiers, used to cringe and wince,
  Poets and harlots, all the throng,
  Let loose their scandal and their song.

Dante at Verona.

No book keeps record if the seat
 Which Dante held at his host's board
 Were sat in next by clerk or lord,—
If leman lolled with dainty feet
 At ease, or hostage brooded there,
 Or priest lacked silence for his prayer.

Eat and wash hands, Can Grande;—scarce
 We know their deeds now: hands which fed
 Our Dante with that bitter bread;
And thou the watch-dog of those stairs
 Which, of all paths his feet knew well,
 Were steeper found than Heaven or Hell.

Dante at Verona.

Tosinghi passed, Manelli passed,
  Rinucci passed, each in his place;
  But not an Alighieri's face
Went by that day from first to last
  In the Republic's triumph; nor
  A foot came home to Dante's door.

(RESPUBLICA—a public thing:
  A shameful, shameless prostitute,
  Whose lust with one lord may not suit,
So takes by turn its revelling
  A night with each, till each at morn
  Is stripped and beaten forth forlorn,

And leaves her, cursing her. If she,
  Indeed, have not some spice-draught, hid
  In scent under a silver lid,
To drench his open throat with—he
  Once hard asleep; and thrust him not
  At dawn beneath the stairs to rot.

Such *this* Republic!—not the Maid
  He yearned for; she who yet should stand
  With Heaven's accepted hand in hand,
Invulnerable and unbetray'd:
  To whom, even as to God should be
  Obeisance one with Liberty.)

Years filled out their twelve moons, and ceased
  One in another; and alway
  There were the whole twelve hours each day
And each night as the years increased;
  And rising moon and setting sun
  Beheld that Dante's work was done.

Dante at Verona.

What of his work for Florence?   Well
  It was, he knew, and well must be.
  Yet evermore her hate's decree
Dwelt in his thought intolerable:—
  His body to be burned,[4]— his soul
  To beat its wings at hope's vain goal.

What of his work for Beatrice?
  Now well-nigh was the third song writ,—
  The stars a third time sealing it
With sudden music of pure peace:
  For echoing thrice the threefold song,
  The unnumbered stars the tone prolong.[5]

Each hour, as then the Vision pass'd,
  He heard the utter harmony
  Of the nine trembling spheres, till she
Bowed her eyes towards him in the last,
  So that all ended with her eyes,
  Hell, Purgatory, Paradise.

"It is my trust, as the years fall,
  To write more worthily of her
  Who now, being made God's minister,
Looks on His visage and knows all."
  Such was the hope that love dar'd blend
  With grief's slow fires, to make an end

Of the "New Life," his youth's dear book:
  Adding thereunto: "In such trust
  I labour, and believe I must
Accomplish this which my soul took
  In charge, if God, my Lord and hers,
  Leave my life with me a few years."

THE MIRROR.

SHE knew it not:—most perfect pain
　To learn: this too she knew not.　Strife
　　For me, calm hers, as from the first.
　　'Twas but another bubble burst
　Upon the curdling draught of life,—
My silent patience mine again.

As who, of forms that crowd unknown
　Within a distant mirror's shade,
　　Deems such an one himself, and makes
　　Some sign; but when the image shakes
　No whit, he finds his thought betray'd,
And must seek elsewhere for his own.

A LAST CONFESSION.

A CRITIC of *The Catholic World*, commenting upon the fact that *A Last Confession* had been compared to Browning's narrative poems of Italian life, says: "It has, indeed, all of Browning's strength, but none of his dense English misconception of Italian character." Mr. Sharp calls it "Rossetti's dramatic *chef-d'œuvre*," and adds: "I do not know in exactly what estimation the author held it himself, but I remember his telling me that about the best review he had ever had 'spoke with justice' of his three chief poems being *A Last Confession, Dante at Verona*, and *The Burden of Nineveh*." When the poem was put in shape for the volume of 1870 Rossetti was much exercised over the criticisms made by his brother upon the little Italian song introduced into the poem. Mr. William Rossetti considered some of the lines lax in metre, according to Italian prosody, but Rossetti maintained that the song was meant to be in "a very irregular antiquated sort of Italian" and contained no worse slips than occur continually among the earliest poets. *A Last Confession* was the first of Rossetti's poems to be translated into Italian, possibly on account of the peculiarly Italian setting of the narrative which refers to the revolutionary movement in Italy before national unity was attained.

A LAST CONFESSION.

(Regno Lombardo-Veneto, 1848.)

1850.

.　　.　　.　　.　　.　　.

OUR Lombard country-girls along the coast
Wear daggers in their garters: for they know
That they might hate another girl to death
Or meet a German lover.　Such a knife
I bought her, with a hilt of horn and pearl.

　Father, you cannot know of all my thoughts
That day in going to meet her, — that last day
For the last time, she said;—of all the love
And all the hopeless hope that she might change
And go back with me.　Ah! and everywhere,
At places we both knew along the road,
Some fresh shape of herself as once she was
Grew present at my side; until it seemed—
So close they gathered round me — they would all
Be with me when I reached the spot at last,
To plead my cause with her against herself
So changed.　O Father, if you knew all this
You cannot know, then you would know too, Father.
And only then, if God can pardon me.
What can be told I'll tell, if you will hear.

　I passed a village-fair upon my road,
And thought, being empty-handed, I would take

A Last Confession.

Some little present: such might prove, I said,
Either a pledge between us, or (God help me!)
A parting gift.   And there it was I bought
The knife I spoke of, such as women wear.

   That day, some three hours afterwards, I found
For certain, it must be a parting gift.
And, standing silent now at last, I looked
Into her scornful face; and heard the sea
Still trying hard to din into my ears
Some speech it knew which still might change her
      heart,
If only it could make me understand.
One moment thus.   Another, and her face
Seemed further off than the last line of sea,
So that I thought, if now she were to speak
I could not hear her.   Then again I knew
All, as we stood together on the sand
At Iglio, in the first thin shade o' the hills.

   "Take it," I said, and held it out to her,
While the hilt glanced within my trembling hold;
"Take it and keep it for my sake," I said.
Her neck unbent not, neither did her eyes
Move, nor her foot left beating of the sand;
Only she put it by from her and laughed.

   Father, you hear my speech and not her laugh;
But God heard that.   Will God remember all?

   It was another laugh than the sweet sound
Which rose from her sweet childish heart, that day
Eleven years before, when first I found her
Alone upon the hill-side; and her curls
Shook down in the warm grass as she looked up

A Last Confession.

Out of her curls in my eyes bent to hers.
She might have served a painter to pourtray
That heavenly child which in the latter days
Shall walk between the lion and the lamb.
I had been for nights in hiding, worn and sick
And hardly fed; and so her words at first
Seemed fitful like the talking of the trees
And voices in the air that knew my name.
And I remember that I sat me down
Upon the slope with her, and thought the world
Must be all over or had never been,
We seemed there so alone. And soon she told me
Her parents both were gone away from her.
I thought perhaps she meant that they had died;
But when I asked her this, she looked again
Into my face and said that yestereve
They kissed her long, and wept and made her weep,
And gave her all the bread they had with them,
And then had gone together up the hill
Where we were sitting now, and had walked on
Into the great red light; "and so," she said,
"I have come up here too; and when this evening
They step out of the light as they stepped in,
I shall be here to kiss them." And she laughed.

Then I bethought me suddenly of the famine;
And how the church-steps throughout all the town,
When last I had been there a month ago,
Swarmed with starved folk; and how the bread was
        weighed
By Austrians armed; and women that I knew
For wives and mothers walked the public street,
Saying aloud that if their husbands feared
To snatch the children's food, themselves would stay

A Last Confession.

Till they had earned it there.   So then this child
Was piteous to me; for all told me then
Her parents must have left her to God's chance,
To man's or to the Church's charity,
Because of the great famine, rather than
To watch her growing thin between their knees.
With that, God took my mother's voice and spoke,
And sights and sounds came back and things long since,
And all my childhood found me on the hills;
And so I took her with me.

                        I was young,
Scarce man then, Father: but the cause which gave
The wounds I die of now had brought me then
Some wounds already; and I lived alone,
As any hiding hunted man must live.
It was no easy thing to keep a child
In safety; for herself it was not safe,
And doubled my own danger: but I knew
That God would help me.

                   Yet a little while
Pardon me, Father, if I pause.   I think
I have been speaking to you of some matters
There was no need to speak of, have I not?
You do not know how clearly those things stood
Within my mind, which I have spoken of,
Nor how they strove for utterance.   Life all past
Is like the sky when the sun sets in it,
Clearest where furthest off.

                 I told you how
She scorned my parting gift and laughed.   And yet
A woman's laugh 's another thing sometimes:
I think they laugh in heaven.   I know last night
I dreamed I saw into the garden of God,
Where women walked whose painted images

A Last Confession.

I have seen with candles round them in the church.
They bent this way and that, one to another,
Playing: and over the long golden hair
Of each there floated like a ring of fire
Which when she stooped stooped with her, and when
      she rose
Rose with her.   Then a breeze flew in among them,
As if a window had been opened in heaven
For God to give His blessing from, before
This world of ours should set; (for in my dream
I thought our world was setting, and the sun
Flared, a spent taper;) and beneath that gust
The rings of light quivered like forest-leaves.
Then all the blessed maidens who were there
Stood up together, as it were a voice
That called them; and they threw their tresses back,
And smote their palms, and all laughed up at once,
For the strong heavenly joy they had in them
To hear God bless the world.   Wherewith I woke:
And looking round, I saw as usual
That she was standing there with her long locks
Pressed to her side; and her laugh ended theirs.

For always when I see her now, she laughs.
And yet her childish laughter haunts me too,
The life of this dead terror; as in days
When she, a child, dwelt with me.   I must tell
Something of those days yet before the end.

I brought her from the city — one such day
When she was still a merry loving child, —
The earliest gift I mind my giving her;
A little image of a flying Love

A Last Confession.

Made of our coloured glass-ware, in his hands
A dart of gilded metal and a torch.
And him she kissed and me, and fain would know
Why were his poor eyes blindfold, why the wings
And why the arrow.   What I knew I told
Of Venus and of Cupid,—strange old tales.
And when she heard that he could rule the loves
Of men and women, still she shook her head
And wondered; and, "Nay, nay," she murmured still,
"So strong, and he a younger child than I!"
And then she'd have me fix him on the wall
Fronting her little bed; and then again
She needs must fix him there herself, because
I gave him to her and she loved him so,
And he should make her love me better yet,
If women loved the more, the more they grew.
But the fit place upon the wall was high
For her, and so I held her in my arms:
And each time that the heavy pruning-hook
I gave her for a hammer slipped away
As it would often, still she laughed and laughed
And kissed and kissed me.   But amid her mirth,
Just as she hung the image on the nail,
It slipped and all its fragments strewed the ground :
And as it fell she screamed, for in her hand
The dart had entered deeply and drawn blood.
And so her laughter turned to tears: and "Oh!"
I said, the while I bandaged the small hand,—
"That I should be the first to make you bleed,
Who love and love and love you!"—kissing still
The fingers till I got her safe to bed.
And still she sobbed,—"not for the pain at all,"
She said, "but for the Love, the poor good Love
You gave me."   So she cried herself to sleep.

A Last Confession.

Another later thing comes back to me.
'T was in those hardest foulest days of all,
When still from his shut palace, sitting clean
Above the splash of blood, old Metternich
(May his soul die, and never-dying worms
Feast on its pain for ever!) used to thin
His year's doomed hundreds daintily, each month
Thirties and fifties.   This time, as I think,
Was when his thrift forbad the poor to take
That evil brackish salt which the dry rocks
Keep all through winter when the sea draws in.
The first I heard of it was a chance shot
In the street here and there, and on the stones
A stumbling clatter as of horse hemmed round.
Then, when she saw me hurry out of doors,
My gun slung at my shoulder and my knife
Stuck in my girdle, she smoothed down my hair
And laughed to see me look so brave, and leaped
Up to my neck and kissed me.   She was still
A child; and yet that kiss was on my lips
So hot all day where the smoke shut us in.

For now, being always with her, the first love
I had — the father's, brother's love — was changed,
I think, in somewise; like a holy thought
Which is a prayer before one knows of it.
The first time I perceived this, I remember,
Was once when after hunting I came home
Weary, and she brought food and fruit for me,
And sat down at my feet upon the floor
Leaning against my side.   But when I felt
Her sweet head reach from that low seat of hers
So high as to be laid upon my heart,
I turned and looked upon my darling there

A Last Confession.

And marked for the first time how tall she was;
And my heart beat with so much violence
Under her cheek, I thought she could not choose
But wonder at it soon and ask me why;
And so I bade her rise and eat with me.
And when, remembering all and counting back
The time, I made out fourteen years for her
And told her so, she gazed at me with eyes
As of the sky and sea on a grey day,
And drew her long hands through her hair, and asked
      me
If she was not a woman; and then laughed:
And as she stooped in laughing, I could see
Beneath the growing throat the breasts half-globed
Like folded lilies deepset in the stream.

   Yes, let me think of her as then; for so
Her image, Father, is not like the sights
Which come when you are gone.   She had a mouth
Made to bring death to life,—the underlip
Sucked in, as if it strove to kiss itself.
Her face was pearly pale, as when one stoops
Over wan water; and the dark crisped hair
And the hair's shadow made it paler still:—
Deep-serried locks, the dimness of the cloud
Where the moon's gaze is set in eddying gloom.
Her body bore her neck as the tree's stem
Bears the top branch; and as the branch sustains
The flower of the year's pride, her high neck bore
That face made wonderful with night and day.
Her voice was swift, yet ever the last words
Fell lingeringly; and rounded finger-tips
She had, that clung a little where they touched
And then were gone o' the instant.   Her great eyes,

A Last Confession.

That sometimes turned half dizzily beneath
The passionate lids, as faint, when she would speak,
Had also in them hidden springs of mirth,
Which under the dark lashes evermore
Shook to her laugh, as when a bird flies low
Between the water and the willow-leaves,
And the shade quivers till he wins the light.

　　I was a moody comrade to her then,
For all the love I bore her.　　Italy,
The weeping desolate mother, long has claimed
Her sons' strong arms to lean on, and their hands
To lop the poisonous thicket from her path,
Cleaving her way to light.　　And from her need
Had grown the fashion of my whole poor life
Which I was proud to yield her, as my father
Had yielded his.　　And this had come to be
A game to play, a love to clasp, a hate
To wreak, all things together that a man
Needs for his blood to ripen; till at times
All else seemed shadows, and I wondered still
To see such life pass muster and be deemed
Time's bodily substance.　　In those hours, no doubt,
To the young girl my eyes were like my soul,—
Dark wells of death-in-life that yearned for day.
And though she ruled me always, I remember
That once when I was thus and she still kept
Leaping about the place and laughing, I
Did almost chide her; whereupon she knelt
And putting her two hands into my breast
Sang me a song.　　Are these tears in my eyes?
'T is long since I have wept for anything.
I thought that song forgotten out of mind;
And now, just as I spoke of it, it came

A Last Confession.

All back.   It is but a rude thing, ill rhymed,
Such as a blind man chaunts and his dog hears
Holding the platter, when the children run
To merrier sport and leave him.   Thus it goes:—

La bella donna
Piangendo disse:
" Come son fisse
Le stelle in cielo!
Quel fiato anelo
Dello stanco sole,
Quanto m' assonna!
E la luna, macchiata
Come uno specchio
Logoro e vecchio,—
Faccia affannata,
Che cosa vuole?

" Chè stelle, luna, e sole,
Ciascun, m' annoja
E m' annojano insieme;
Non me ne preme
Nè ci prendo gioja.
E veramente,
Che le spalle sien franche
E le braccia bianche
E il seno caldo e tondo,
Non mi fa niente.
Che cosa al mondo
Posso più far di questi
Se non piacciono a te, come di-
   cesti? "

La donna rise
E riprese ridendo:—
" Questa mano che prendo
È dunque mia?
Tu m' ami dunque?
Dimmelo ancora
Non in modo qualunque,
Ma le parole
Belle e precise
Che dicesti pria.

' Siccome suole
La state talora

She wept, sweet lady,
And said in weeping:
" What spell is keeping
The stars so steady?
Why does the power
Of the sun's noon-hour
To sleep so move me?
And the moon in heaven,
Stained where she passes
As a worn-out glass is,—
Wearily driven,
Why walks she above me?

" Stars, moon, and sun too,
I 'm tired of either
And all together!
Whom speak they unto
That I should listen?
For very surely,
Though my arms and shoulders
Dazzle beholders,
And my eyes glisten,
All 's nothing purely!
What are words said for
At all about them,
If he they are made for
Can do without them? "

She laughed, sweet lady,
And said in laughing:
" His hand clings half in
My own already!
Oh! do you love me?
Oh! speak of passion
In no new fashion,
No loud inveighings,
But the old sayings
You once said of me.

" You said: ' As summer,
Through boughs grown brittle,

A Last Confession.

(Dicesti) *un qualche istante*
Tornare innanzi inverno,
Così tu fai ch' io scerno
Le foglie tutte quante,
Ben ch' io certo tenessi
Per passato l' autunno.'

" Eccolo il mio alunno!
lo debbo insegnargli
Quei cari detti istessi
Ch' ei mi disse una volta!
Oimè!   Che cosa dargli,"
(Ma ridea piano piano
Dei baci in sulla mano,)
" Ch' ei non m'abbia da lungo
   tempo tolta ? "

Comes back a little
Ere frosts benumb her,—
So bring'st thou to me
All leaves and flowers,
Though autumn 's gloomy
To-day in the bowers.'

" Oh! does he love me,
When my voice teaches
The very speeches
He then spoke of me ?
Alas! what flavour
Still with me lingers ? "
(But she laughs as my kisses
Glowed in her fingers
With love's old blisses.)
" Oh! what one favour
Remains to woo him,
Whose whole poor savour
Belongs not to him ? "

That I should sing upon this bed!—with you
To listen, and such words still left to say!
Yet was it I that sang ?   The voice seemed hers,
As on the very day she sang to me;
When, having done, she took out of my hand
Something that I had played with all the while
And laid it down beyond my reach; and so
Turning my face round till it fronted hers,—
" Weeping or laughing, which was best ? " she said.

But these are foolish tales.   How should I show
The heart that glowed then with love's heat, each day
More and more brightly ?—when for long years now
The very flame that flew about the heart,
And gave it fiery wings, has come to be
The lapping blaze of hell's environment
Whose tongues all bid the molten heart despair.

Yet one more thing comes back on me to-night
Which I may tell you: for it bore my soul

A Last Confession.

Dread firstlings of the brood that rend it now.
It chanced that in our last year's wanderings
We dwelt at Monza, far away from home,
If home we had: and in the Duomo there
I sometimes entered with her when she prayed.
An image of Our Lady stands there, wrought
In marble by some great Italian hand
In the great days when she and Italy
Sat on one throne together: and to her
And to none else my loved one told her heart.
She was a woman then; and as she knelt,—
Her sweet brow in the sweet brow's shadow there,—
They seemed two kindred forms whereby our land
(Whose work still serves the world for miracle)
Made manifest herself in womanhood.
Father, the day I speak of was the first
For weeks that I had borne her company
Into the Duomo; and those weeks had been
Much troubled, for then first the glimpses came
Of some impenetrable restlessness
Growing in her to make her changed and cold.
And as we entered there that day, I bent
My eyes on the fair Image, and I said
Within my heart, "Oh turn her heart to me!"
And so I left her to her prayers, and went
To gaze upon the pride of Monza's shrine,
Where in the sacristy the light still falls
Upon the Iron Crown of Italy,
On whose crowned heads the day has closed, nor yet
The daybreak gilds another head to crown.
But coming back, I wondered when I saw
That the sweet Lady of her prayers now stood
Alone without her; until further off,
Before some new Madonna gaily decked,

A Last Confession.

Tinselled and gewgawed, a slight German toy,
I saw her kneel, still praying. At my step
She rose, and side by side we left the church.
I was much moved, and sharply questioned her
Of her transferred devotion; but she seemed
Stubborn and heedless; till she lightly laughed
And said: "The old Madonna? Aye indeed,
She had my old thoughts,—this one has my new."
Then silent to the soul I held my way:
And from the fountains of the public place
Unto the pigeon-haunted pinnacles,
Bright wings and water winnowed the bright air;
And stately with her laugh's subsiding smile
She went, with clear-swayed waist and towering neck
And hands held light before her; and the face
Which long had made a day in my life's night
Was night in day to me; as all men's eyes
Turned on her beauty, and she seemed to tread
Beyond my heart to the world made for her.

Ah, there! my wounds will snatch my sense again:
The pain comes billowing on like a full cloud
Of thunder, and the flash that breaks from it
Leaves my brain burning. That's the wound he gave,
The Austrian whose white coat I still made match
With his white face, only the two grew red[1]
As suits his trade. The devil makes them wear
White for a livery, that the blood may show
Braver that brings them to him. So he looks
Sheer o'er the field and knows his own at once.

Give me a draught of water in that cup;
My voice feels thick; perhaps you do not hear;
But you *must* hear. If you mistake my words

[159]

A Last Confession.

And so absolve me, I am sure the blessing
Will burn my soul. If you mistake my words
And so absolve me, Father, the great sin
Is yours, not mine: mark this: your soul shall burn
With mine for it. I have seen pictures where
Souls burned with Latin shriekings in their mouths:
Shall my end be as theirs? Nay, but I know
'T is you shall shriek in Latin. Some bell rings,
Rings through my brain: it strikes the hour in hell.

　　You see I cannot, Father; I have tried,
But cannot, as you see. These twenty times
Beginning, I have come to the same point
And stopped. Beyond, there are but broken words
Which will not let you understand my tale.
It is that then we have her with us here,
As when she wrung her hair out in my dream
To-night, till all the darkness reeked of it.
Her hair is always wet, for she has kept
Its tresses wrapped about her side for years;
And when she wrung them round over the floor,
I heard the blood between her fingers hiss;
So that I sat up in my bed and screamed
Once and again; and once to once, she laughed.
Look that you turn not now,—she 's at your back:
Gather your robe up, Father, and keep close,
Or she 'll sit down on it and send you mad.

　　At Iglio in the first thin shade o' the hills
The sand is black and red. The black was black
When what was spilt that day sank into it.
And the red scarcely darkened. There I stood
This night with her, and saw the sand the same.

A Last Confession.

What would you have me tell you? Father, father,
How shall I make you know? You have not known
The dreadful soul of woman, who one day
Forgets the old and takes the new to heart,
Forgets what man remembers, and therewith
Forgets the man. Nor can I clearly tell
How the change happened between her and me.
Her eyes looked on me from an emptied heart
When most my heart was full of her; and still
In every corner of myself I sought
To find what service failed her; and no less
Than in the good time past, there all was hers.
What do you love? Your Heaven? Conceive it spread
For one first year of all eternity
All round you with all joys and gifts of God;
And then when most your soul is blent with it
And all yields song together,—then it stands
O' the sudden like a pool that once gave back
Your image, but now drowns it and is clear
Again,—or like a sun bewitched, that burns
Your shadow from you, and still shines in sight.
How could you bear it? Would you not cry out,
Among those eyes grown blind to you, those ears
That hear no more your voice you hear the same,—
"God! what is left but hell for company,
But hell, hell, hell?"—until the name so breathed
Whirled with hot wind and sucked you down in fire?
Even so I stood the day her empty heart
Left her place empty in our home, while yet
I knew not why she went nor where she went
Nor how to reach her: so I stood the day
When to my prayers at last one sight of her
Was granted, and I looked on heaven made pale
With scorn, and heard heaven mock me in that laugh.

A Last Confession.

O sweet, long sweet! Was that some ghost of you,
Even as your ghost that haunts me now,—twin shapes
Of fear and hatred? May I find you yet
Mine when death wakes? Ah! be it even in flame,
We may have sweetness yet, if you but say
As once in childish sorrow: "Not my pain,
My pain was nothing: oh your poor poor love,
Your broken love!"

      My Father, have I not
Yet told you the last things of that last day
On which I went to meet her by the sea?
O God, O God! but I must tell you all.

Midway upon my journey, when I stopped
To buy the dagger at the village fair,
I saw two cursed rats about the place
I knew for spies—blood-sellers both. That day
Was not yet over; for three hours to come
I prized my life: and so I looked around
For safety. A poor painted mountebank
Was playing tricks and shouting in a crowd.
I knew he must have heard my name, so I
Pushed past and whispered to him who I was,
And of my danger. Straight he hustled me
Into his booth, as it were in the trick,
And brought me out next minute with my face
All smeared in patches and a zany's gown;
And there I handed him his cups and balls
And swung the sand-bags round to clear the ring
For half an hour. The spies came once and looked;
And while they stopped, and made all sights and sounds
Sharp to my startled senses, I remember
A woman laughed above me. I looked up
And saw where a brown-shouldered harlot leaned

A Last Confession.

Half through a tavern window thick with vine.
Some man had come behind her in the room
And caught her by her arms, and she had turned
With that coarse empty laugh on him, as now
He munched her neck with kisses, while the vine
Crawled in her back.

               And three hours afterwards,
When she that I had run all risks to meet
Laughed as I told you, my life burned to death
Within me, for I thought it like the laugh
Heard at the fair. She had not left me long;
But all she might have changed to, or might change to,
(I know nought since—she never speaks a word—)
Seemed in that laugh. Have I not told you yet,
Not told you all this time what happened, Father,
When I had offered her the little knife,
And bade her keep it for my sake that loved her,
And she had laughed ? Have I not told you yet ?

  "Take it," I said to her the second time,
"Take it and keep it." And then came a fire
That burnt my hand; and then the fire was blood,
And sea and sky were blood and fire, and all
The day was one red blindness; till it seemed,[2]
Within the whirling brain's eclipse, that she
Or I or all things bled or burned to death.
And then I found her laid against my feet
And knew that I had stabbed her, and saw still
Her look in falling. For she took the knife
Deep in her heart, even as I bade her then,
And fell; and her stiff bodice scooped the sand
Into her bosom.

              And she keeps it, see,
Do you not see she keeps it ?—there, beneath

A Last Confession.

Wet fingers and wet tresses, in her heart.
For look you, when she stirs her hand, it shows
The little hilt of horn and pearl,—even such
A dagger as our women of the coast
Twist in their garters.

                Father, I have done:
And from her side she now unwinds the thick
Dark hair; all round her side it is wet through,
But, like the sand at Iglio, does not change.
Now you may see the dagger clearly.   Father,
I have told all: tell me at once what hope
Can reach me still.   For now she draws it out
Slowly, and only smiles as yet: look, Father,
She scarcely smiles: but I shall hear her laugh
Soon, when she shows the crimson steel⁹ to God.

A YOUNG FIR-WOOD.

(Between Ightham and Sevenoaks, November, 1850.)

THESE little firs to-day are things
　　To clasp into a giant's cap,
　　Or fans to suit his lady's lap.
From many winters many springs
　　Shall cherish them in strength and sap
　　Till they be marked upon the map,
A wood for the wind's wanderings.

All seed is in the sower's hands:
　　And what at first was trained to spread
　　Its shelter for some single head,—
Yea, even such fellowship of wands,—
　　May hide the sunset, and the shade
　　Of its great multitude be laid
Upon the earth and elder sands.

Mary Magdalen at the Door of Simon
the Pharisee.
Pen and ink. 1858

INTRODUCTION TO THE BURDEN
OF NINEVEH.

R OSSETTI, watching some of the Nineveh sculptures
unpacked at the Museum in London, received
from them his suggestion for this poem,— one of the very
few in which he meditates at length upon mankind in
general, their faiths, and the vagaries of their fortunes.
Ruskin was mightily impressed by the poem and wrote
with characteristic ecstasy and humility to Rossetti:

"I am wild to know who is the author of *The Burden
of Nineveh,* in No. 8 of *Oxford and Cambridge.* It is
glorious. Please find out for me and see if I can get
acquainted with him."

Rossetti must, of course, have replied that he was the
author, and one instinctively laments for Ruskin the loss
of a new idol on whom to heap praise and patronage. -

The Oxford and Cambridge version was very differ-
ent from the later versions, and will be interesting to
students of Rossetti's careful methods in revision.

The following five lines belong to the original draft of
the poem, and Rossetti thought of restoring them in the
1870 volume, but finally concluded to leave them out,
remembering that "Brown once suggested difficulties
about the shells, bells, etc.— could they be heard under
the earth? Were there any to be heard, etc."

"How much of Heaven's thunder — how much else
Man's puny roar?—what cry of shells
Cleft amid leaguered citadels —
How many lordships loud with bells
Heardst thou in secret Nineveh?"

OXFORD AND CAMBRIDGE VERSION
OF THE BURDEN OF NINEVEH.

" Burden. Heavy calamity; the chorus of a song."—*Dictionary.*

I HAVE no taste for polyglot:
At the Museum 't was my lot,
Just once, to jot and blot and rot
In Babel for I know not what.
  I went at two, I left at three.
Round those still floors I tramp'd, to win
By the great porch the dirt and din;
And as I made the last door spin
And issued, they were hoisting in
  A wingèd beast from Nineveh.

A human face the creature wore,
And hoofs behind and hoofs before,
And flanks with dark runes fretted o'er.
'T was bull, 't was mitred minotaur;
  A dead disbowell'd mystery;
The mummy of a buried faith,
Stark from the charnel without scathe,
Its wings stood for the light to bathe,—
Such fossil cerements as might swathe
  The very corpse of Nineveh.

Some colour'd Arab straw-matting,
Half-ripp'd, was still upon the thing.
(What song did the brown maidens sing,
From purple mouths alternating,
  When that was woven languidly ?)

[168]

The Burden of Nineveh.

What vows, what rites, what prayers preferr'd,
What songs has the strange image heard?
In what blind vigil stood interr'd
For ages, till an English word
     Broke silence first at Nineveh?

On London stones our sun anew
The beast's recover'd shadow threw
No shade that plague of darkness knew,
No light, no shade, while older grew
     By ages the old earth and sea.
Oh! seem'd it not — that spell once broke,
As though the sculptured warriors woke
As though the shaft the string forsook,
The cymbals clash'd, the chariots shook,
     And there was life in Nineveh?

On London stones its shape lay scored,
That day when, nigh the gates, the Lord
Shelter'd His Jonah with a gourd,
This sun (I said) here present, pour'd
     Even thus this shadow that I see.
This shadow has been shed the same
From sun and moon,—from lamps which came
For prayer,— from fifteen days of flame,
The last, while smoulder'd to a name
     Sardanapalus' Nineveh.

Within thy shadow, haply, once
Sennacherib has knelt, whose sons
Smote him between the altar-stones:
Or pale Semiramis her zones
     Of gold, her incense brought to thee,
In love for grace, in war for aid; . . .
Ay, and who else? . . . till 'neath thy shade
Within his trenches newly made
Last year the Christian knelt and pray'd —
     Not to thy strength — in Nineveh.

The Burden of Nineveh.

Now, thou poor god, within this hall
Where the blank windows blind the wall
From pedestal to pedestal,
The kind of light shall on thee fall
   Which London takes the day to be.
Here cold-pinch'd clerks on yellow days
Shall stop and peer; and in sun-haze
Small clergy crimp their eyes to gaze;
And misses titter in their stays,
   Just fresh from " Layard's Nineveh."

Here, while the Antique-students lunch,
Shall Art be slang'd o'er cheese and hunch,
Whether the great R.A.'s a bunch
Of gods or dogs, and whether Punch
   Is right about the P. R. B.?
Here school-foundations in the act
Of holiday, three files compact
Shall learn to view thee as a fact
Connected with that zealous tract,
   " Rome: Babylon and Nineveh."

Deem'd they of this, those worshippers,
When, in some mythic chain of verse,
Which man shall not again rehearse,
The faces of thy ministers
   Yearn'd pale with bitter ecstasy?
Greece, Egypt, Rome,—did any god
Before whose feet men knelt unshod,
Deem that in this unblest abode
An elder, scarce more unknown god,
   Should house with him from Nineveh?

Ah ! in what quarries lay the stone
From which this pigmy pile has grown,
Unto man's need how long unknown,
Since thy vast temple, court and cone
   Rose far in desert history?

The Burden of Nineveh.

Ah! what is here that does not lie
All strange to thine awaken'd eye?
Ah! what is here can testify,
(Save that dumb presence of the sky)
      Unto thy day and Nineveh?

Why, of those mummies in the room
Above, there might indeed have come
One out of Egypt to thy home,
A pilgrim.   Nay, but even to some
      Of these thou wert antiquity!
And now, they and their gods and thou,
All relics here together,—now
Whose profit? Whether bull or cow,
Isis or Ibis, who or how,
      Whether of Thebes or Nineveh?

The consecrated metals found,
And ivory tablets, underground,—
Wing'd teraphim and creatures crown'd,—
When air and daylight fill'd the mound,
      Fell into dust immediately.
And even as these, the images
Of awe and worship,—even as these,—
So, smitten with the sun's increase,
Her glory mouldered and did cease
      From immemorial Nineveh.

The day her builders made their halt,
      Those cities of the lake of salt
Stood firmly stablish'd without fault,
Made proud with pillars of basalt,
      With sardonyx and porphyry.
The day that Jonah bore abroad
To Nineveh the voice of God,
Beside a brackish lake he trod
Where erst Pride fix'd her sure abode,
      As then in royal Nineveh.

The Burden of Nineveh.

The day when he, Pride's Lord and Man's,
Show'd all earth's kingdoms at a glance
To Him before whose countenance
The years recede, the years advance,
    And said, Fall down and worship me;
'Mid all the pomp beneath that look,
Then stirr'd there, haply, some rebuke,
When to the wind the salt pools shook,
And in those tracts, of life forsook,
    That knew thee not, O Nineveh!

Delicate harlot,—eldest grown
Of earthly queens!   thou on thy throne
In state for ages sat'st alone;
And need were years and lustres flown
    Ere strength of man could vanquish thee:
Whom even thy victor foes must bring
Still royal, among maids that sing
As with doves' voices, taboring
Upon their breasts, unto the King,—
    A kingly conquest, Nineveh!

. . . Here woke my thought.   The wind's slow sway
Had wax'd; and like the human play
Of scorn that smiling spreads away,
The sunshine shiver'd off the day:
The callous wind, it seem'd to me,
Swept up the shadow from the ground:
And pale, as whom the Fates astound
The god forlorn stood wing'd and crown'd:
Within I knew the cry lay bound
    Of the dumb soul of Nineveh.

Then waking up, I turn'd, because
That day my spirits might not pause
O'er any dead thing's doleful laws;
That day all hope with glad applause
    Through miles of London beckon'd me.

The Burden of Nineveh.

And all the wealth of life's free choice,
Love's ardour, friendship's equipoise,
And Ellen's gaze and Philip's voice,
And all that evening's curtain joys,
  Struck pale my dream of Nineveh.

Yet while I walk'd, my sense half shut
Still saw the crowds of kerb and rut
Go past as marshall'd to the strut
Of ranks in gypsum quaintly cut.
  It seem'd in one same pageantry
They follow'd forms which had been erst;
To pass, till on my sight should burst
That future of the best or worst
When some may question which was first,
  Of London or of Nineveh.

For as that Bull-god once did stand
And watch'd the burial-clouds of sand,
Till these at last without a hand
Rose o'er his eyes, another land,
  And blinded him with destiny:
So may he stand again; till now,
In ships of unknown sail and prow,
Some tribe of the Australian plough
Bear him afar, a relic now
  Of London, not of Nineveh.

Or it may chance indeed that when
Man's age is hoary among men,
His centuries threescore and ten,—
His furthest childhood shall seem then
  More clear than later times may be:
Who finding in this desert place
This form, shall hold us for some race
  That walk'd not in Christ's lowly ways,
But bow'd its pride and vow'd its praise
  Unto the god of Nineveh.

The Burden of Nineveh.

The smile rose first,—anon drew nigh
The thought: . . . Those heavy wings spread high
So sure of flight, which do not fly;
That set gaze never on the sky;
     Those scriptured flanks it cannot see;
Its crown, a brow-contracting load;
Its planted feet which trust the sod: . . .
(So grew the image as I trod)
O Nineveh, was this thy God,
     Thine also, mighty Nineveh?

THE BURDEN OF NINEVEH.[1]

In our Museum galleries
To-day I lingered o'er the prize
Dead Greece vouchsafes to living eyes,—
Her art for ever in fresh wise
  From hour to hour rejoicing me.
Sighing I turned at last to win
Once more the London dirt and din;
And as I made the swing-door spin
And issued, they were hoisting in
  A wingèd beast from Nineveh.

A human face the creature wore,
And hoofs behind and hoofs before,
And flanks with dark runes fretted o'er.
'T was bull, 't was mitred Minotaur,
  A dead disbowelled mystery:
The mummy of a buried faith
Stark from the charnel without scathe,
Its wings stood for the light to bathe,—
Such fossil cerements as might swathe
  The very corpse of Nineveh.

The print of its first rush-wrapping,
Wound ere it dried, still ribbed the thing.
What song did the brown maidens sing,
From purple mouths alternating,
  When that was woven languidly?

The Burden of Nineveh.

What vows, what rights, what prayers preferr'd,
What songs has the strange image heard?
In what blind vigil stood interr'd
For ages, till an English word
    Broke silence first at Nineveh?

Oh, when upon each sculptured court,
Where even the wind might not resort,—
O'er which Time passed, of like import
With the wild Arab boys at sport,—
    A living face looked in to see :—
Oh, seemed it not—the spell once broke—
As though the carven warriors woke,
As though the shaft the string forsook,
The symbols clashed, the chariots shook,
    And there was life in Nineveh?

On London stones our sun anew
The beast's recovered shadow threw.
(No shade that plague of darkness knew,
No light, no shade, while older grew
    By ages the old earth and sea.)
Lo thou! could all thy priests have shown
Such proof to make thy godhead known?
From their dead Past thou liv'st alone;
And still thy shadow is thine own,
    Even as of yore in Nineveh.

That day whereof we keep record,
When near thy city-gates the Lord
Sheltered His Jonah with a gourd,
This sun, (I said) here present, pour'd
    Even thus this shadow that I see.

The Burden of Nineveh.

This shadow has been shed the same
From sun and moon,—from lamps which came
For prayer,—from fifteen days of flame,
The last, while smouldered to a name
   Sardanapalus' Nineveh.

Within thy shadow, haply, once
Sennacherib has knelt, whose sons
Smote him between the altar-stones:
Or pale Semiramis her zones
   Of gold, her incense brought to thee,
In love for grace, in war for aid: . . .
Ay, and who else? . . . till 'neath thy shade
Within his trenches newly made
Last year the Christian knelt and pray'd—
   Not to thy strength — in Nineveh.[1]

Now, thou poor god, within this hall
Where the blank windows blind the wall
From pedestal to pedestal,
The kind of light shall on thee fall
   Which London takes the day to be:
While school-foundations in the act
Of holiday, three files compact,
Shall learn to view thee as a fact
Connected with that zealous tract:
   "ROME,— Babylon and Nineveh."

Deemed they of this, those worshipers,
When, in some mythic chain of verse
Which man shall not again rehearse,
The faces of thy ministers
   Yearned pale with bitter ecstasy?

The Burden of Nineveh.

Greece, Egypt, Rome,—did any god
Before whose feet men knelt unshod
Deem that in this unblest abode
Another scarce more unknown god
   Should house with him, from Nineveh?

Ah! in what quarries lay the stone
From which this pillared pile has grown,
Unto man's need how long unknown,
Since those thy temples, court and cone,
   Rose far in desert history?
Ah! what is here that does not lie
All strange to thine awakened eye?
Ah! what is here can testify
(Save that dumb presence of the sky)
   Unto thy day and Nineveh?

Why, of those mummies in the room
Above, there might indeed have come
One out of Egypt to thy home,
An alien.   Nay, but were not some
   Of these thine own "antiquity"?
And now,—they and their gods and thou
All relics here together,—now
Whose profit? whether bull or cow,
Isis or Ibis, who or how,
   Whether of Thebes or Nineveh?

The consecrated metals found,
And ivory tablets, underground,
Winged teraphim and creatures crown'd,
When air and daylight filled the mound,
   Fell into dust immediately.

The Burden of Nineveh.

And even as these, the images
Of awe and worship,—even as these,—
So, smitten with the sun's increase,
Her glory mouldered and did cease
   From immemorial Nineveh.

The day her builders made their halt,
Those cities of the lake of salt
Stood firmly 'stablished without fault,
Made proud with pillars of basalt,
   With sardonyx and porphyry.
The day that Jonah bore abroad
To Nineveh the voice of God,
A brackish lake lay in his road,
Where erst Pride fixed her sure abode,
   As then in royal Nineveh.

The day when he, Pride's lord and Man's,
Showed all the kingdoms at a glance
To Him before whose countenance
The years recede, the years advance,
   And said, Fall down and worship me:—
'Mid all the pomp beneath that look,
Then stirred there, haply, some rebuke,
Where to the wind the Salt Pools shook,
And in those tracts, of life forsook,
   That knew thee not, O Nineveh!

Delicate harlot! On thy throne
Thou with a world beneath thee prone
In state for ages sat'st alone;
And needs were years and lustres flown
   Ere strength of man could vanquish thee:

The Burden of Nineveh.

Whom even thy victor foes must bring,
Still royal, among maids that sing
As with doves' voices, taboring
Upon their breasts, unto the King,—
   A kingly conquest, Nineveh!

. . . Here woke my thought.   The wind's
     slow sway
Had wax'd; and like the human play
Of scorn that smiling spreads away,
The sunshine shiver'd off the day:
   The callous wind, it seem'd to me,
Swept up the shadow from the ground:
And pale as whom the Fates astound,
The god forlorn stood wing'd and crown'd:
Within I knew the cry lay bound
   Of the dumb soul of Nineveh.

And as I turned, my sense half shut
Still saw the crowds of kerb and rut
Go past as marshall'd to the strut
Of ranks in gypsum quaintly cut.
   It seemed in one same pageantry
They follow'd forms which had been erst;
To pass, till on my sight should burst
That future of the best or worst
When some may question which was first,
   Of London or of Nineveh.

For as that Bull-god once did stand
And watched the burial-clouds of sand,
Till these at last without a hand
Rose o'er his eyes, another land,
   And blinded him with destiny:

[180]

The Burden of Nineveh.

So may he stand again; till now,
In ships of unknown sail and prow,
Some tribe of the Australian plough
Bear him afar, a relic now
   Of London, not of Nineveh!

Or it may chance indeed that when
Man's age is hoary among men,
His centuries threescore and ten,—
His furthest childhood shall seem then
   More clear than later times may be:
Who, finding in this desert place
This form, shall hold us for some race
That walked not in Christ's lowly ways,
But bow'd its pride and vow'd its praise
   Unto the God of Nineveh.

The smile rose first,— anon drew nigh
The thought: . . .   Those heavy wings
     spread high,
So sure of flight, which do not fly;
That set gaze never on the sky;
   Those scriptured flanks it cannot see;
Its crown, a brow-contracting load;
Its planted feet which trust the sod: . . .
(So grew the image as I trod:)
O Nineveh, was this thy God,—
   Thine also, mighty Nineveh?

THE CHURCH-PORCH.[1]

Sister, first shake we off the dust we have
   Upon our feet, lest it defile the stones
   Inscriptured, covering their sacred bones
Who lie i' the aisles which keep the names they gave,
Their trust abiding round them in the grave;
   Whom painters paint for visible orisons,
   And to whom sculptors pray in stone and bronze;
Their voices echo still like a spent wave.

Without here, the church-bells are but a tune,
And on the carven church-door this hot noon
   Lays all its heavy sunshine here without:
But having entered in, we shall find there
Silence, and sudden dimness, and deep prayer,
   And faces of crowned angels all about.

WELLINGTON'S FUNERAL.[1]

18th November, 1852.

"VICTORY!"
So once more the cry must be.
Duteous mourning we fulfil
In God's name; but by God's will,
Doubt not, the last word is still
"Victory!"

Funeral,
In the music round this pall,
Solemn grief yields earth to earth;
But what tones of solemn mirth
In the pageant of new birth
Rise and fall?

For indeed,
If our eyes were openèd,
Who shall say what escort floats
Here, which breath nor gleam denotes,—
Fiery horses, chariots
Fire-footed?

Trumpeter,
Even thy call he may not hear;
Long-known voice for ever past,
Till with one more trumpet-blast
God's assuring word at last
Reach his ear.

[183]

Wellington's Funeral.

Multitude,
Hold your breath in reverent mood:
For while earth's whole kindred stand
Mute even thus on either hand,
This soul's labour shall be scann'd
    And found good.

Cherubim,
Lift ye not even now your hymn?
Lo! once lent for human lack,
Michael's sword is rendered back.
Thrills not now the starry track,
    Seraphim?

Gabriel,
Since the gift of thine "All hail!"
Out of Heaven no time hath brought
Gift with fuller blessing fraught
Than the peace which this man wrought
    Passing well.

Be no word
Raised of bloodshed Christ abhorr'd.
Say: "'T was thus in His decrees
Who Himself, the Prince of Peace,
For His harvest's high increase
    Sent a sword."

Veterans,
He by whom the neck of France
Then was given unto your heel,
Timely sought, may lend as well
To your sons his terrible
    Countenance.

Wellington's Funeral.

Waterloo!
As the last grave must renew,
Ere fresh death, the banshee-strain,—
So methinks upon thy plain
Falls some presage in the rain,
  In the dew.

And O thou,
Watching with an exile's brow
Unappeased, o'er death's dumb flood:—
Lo! the saving strength of God
In some new heart's English blood
  Slumbers now.

Emperor,
Is this all thy work was for?—
Thus to see thy self-sought aim,
Yea thy titles, yea thy name,
In another's shame, to shame
  Bandied o'er?[1]

Wellington,
Thy great work is but begun.
With quick seed his end is rife
Whose long tale of conquering strife
Shows no triumph like his life
  Lost and won.

INTRODUCTION TO "STRATTON WATER."

IN this one instance only in the course of his ballad-writing did Rossetti attempt closely to conform to the old ballad type. We find him defending *Stratton Water* from certain strictures by William Allingham as follows:

"Many thanks for your minute criticism on my ballad, which was just of the kind I wanted. Not, of course, that a British poet is going to knock under on all points,—accordingly, I take care to disagree from you in various respects — as regards abruptnesses, improbabilities, prosaicisms, coarsenesses, and other *esses* and *isms,* not more prominent, I think, in my production than in its models. As to dialect there is much to be said, but I doubt much whether, as you say, mine is more Scotticised than many or even the majority of genuine old ballads."

Before publishing *Stratton Water* in the volume of 1870, Rossetti added to the original draft three stanzas after the line, "The nags were in the stall," to give the gradual impression of Lord Sands's recognising the girl whom he thought dead; and a further stanza,— "about the priest in a funk" to use Rossetti's own expressive phrase.

STRATTON WATER.

"O HAVE you seen the Stratton flood
  That 's great with rain to-day?
It runs beneath your wall, Lord Sands,
  Full of the new-mown hay.

"I led your hounds to Hutton bank
  To bathe at early morn:
They got their bath by Borrowbrake
  Above the standing corn."

Out from the castle-stair Lord Sands
  Looked up the western lea;
The rook was grieving on her nest,
  The flood was round her tree.

Over the castle-wall Lord Sands
  Looked down the eastern hill:
The stakes swam free among the boats,
  The flood was rising still.

"What 's yonder far below that lies
  So white against the slope?"
"O it 's a sail o' your bonny barks
  The waters have washed up."

"But I have never a sail so white,
  And the water 's is not yet there."
"O it 's the swans o' your bonny lake
  The rising flood doth scare."

Stratton Water.

7.
　　"The swans they would not hold so still,
　　　So high they would not win."
　　"O it 's Joyce my wife has spread her smock
　　　And fears to fetch it in."

8
　　"Nay, knave, it 's neither sail nor swans,
　　　Nor aught that you can say;
　　For though your wife might leave her smock,
　　　Herself she 'd bring away."

　　Lord Sands has passed the turret-stair,
　　　The court, and yard, and all;
　　The kine were in the byre that day,
　　　The nags were in the stall.

10
　　Lord Sands has won the weltering slope
　　　Whereon the white shape lay:
　　The clouds were still above the hill,
　　　And the shape was still as they.

　　Oh pleasant is the gaze of life
　　　And sad is death's blind head;
　　But awful are the living eyes
　　　In the face of one thought dead!

12
　　"In God's name, Janet, is it me
　　　Thy ghost has come to seek?"
　　"Nay, wait another hour, Lord Sands,—
　　　Be sure my ghost shall speak."

　　A moment stood he as a stone,
　　　Then grovelled to his knee.
　　"O Janet, O my love, my love,
　　　Rise up and come with me!"
　　"O once before you bade me come,
　　　And it 's here you have brought me!

Stratton Water.

14 "O many 's the sweet word, Lord Sands,
      You 've spoken oft to me;
    But all that I have from you to-day
      Is the rain on my body.

15 "And many 's the good gift, Lord Sands,
      You 've promised oft to me;
    But the gift of yours I keep to-day
      Is the babe in my body.

16 "O it 's not in any earthly bed
      That first my babe I 'll see;
    For I have brought my body here
      That the flood may cover me."

17 His face was close against her face,
      His hands of hers were fain:
    O her wet cheeks were hot with tears,
      Her wet hands cold with rain.

18 "They told me you were dead, Janet,—
      How could I guess the lie?"
    "They told me you were false, Lord Sands,—
      What could I do but die?"

19 "Now keep you well, my brother Giles,—
      Through you I deemed her dead!
    As wan as your towers seem to-day,
      To-morrow they 'll be red.

20 "Look down, look down, my false mother,
      That bade me not to grieve:
    You 'll look up when our marriage fires
      Are lit to-morrow eve:

Stratton Water.

21   "O more than one and more than two
         The sorrow of this shall see:
      But it 's to-morrow, love, for them,—
         To-day 's for thee and me."

22   He 's drawn her face between his hands
         And her pale mouth to his:
      No bird that was so still that day
         Chirps sweeter than his kiss.

23   The flood was creeping round their feet.
         "O Janet, come away!
      The hall is warm for the marriage-rite,
         The bed for the birthday."

      "Nay, but I hear your mother cry,
         'Go bring this bride to bed!
      And would she christen her babe unborn,
         So wet she comes to wed?'

25   "I 'll be your wife to cross your door
         And meet your mother's e'e.
      We plighted troth to wed i' the kirk,
         And it 's there you 'll wed with me."

26   He 's ta'en her by the short girdle
         And by the dripping sleeve:
      "Go fetch Sir Jock my mother's priest,—
         You 'll ask of him no leave.

27   "O it 's one half-hour to reach the kirk
         And one for the marriage-rite;
      And kirk and castle and castle-lands
         Shall be our babe's to-night."

Stratton Water.

29   "The flood's in the kirkyard, Lord Sands,
         And round the belfry-stair."
      "I bade you fetch the priest," he said,
         "Myself shall bring him there.

29   "It's for the lilt of wedding bells
         We'll have the hail to pour,
      And for the clink of bridle-reins
         The plashing of the oar."

30   Beneath them on the nether hill
         A boat was floating wide:
      Lord Sands swam out and caught the oars
         And rowed to the hill-side.

31   He's wrapped her in a green mantle
         And set her softly in;
      Her hair was wet upon her face,
         Her face was grey and thin;
      And "Oh!" she said, "lie still, my babe,
         It's out you must not win!"

32   But woe's my heart for Father John
         As hard as he might pray,
      There seemed no help but Noah's ark
         Or Jonah's fish that day.

33   The first strokes that the oars struck
         Were over the broad leas;
      The next strokes that the oars struck
         They pushed beneath the trees;

34   The last stroke that the oars struck,
         The good boat's head was met,
      And there the gate of the kirkyard
         Stood like a ferry-gate.

Stratton Water.

35   He 's set his hand upon the bar
        And lightly leaped within:
    He 's lifted her to his left shoulder,
        Her knees beside his chin.

36   The graves lay deep beneath the flood
        Under the rain alone;
    And when the foot-stone made him slip,
        He held by the head-stone.

37   The empty boat thrawed i' the wind,
        Against the postern tied.
    "Hold still, you 've brought my love with me,
        You shall take back my bride."

38   But woe 's my heart for Father John
        And the saints he clamoured to!
    There 's never a saint but Christopher
        Might hale such buttocks through!

39   And "Oh!" she said, "on men's shoulders
        I well had thought to wend,
    And well to travel with a priest,
        But not to have cared or ken'd.

40   "And oh!" she said, " it 's well this way
        That I thought to have fared,—
    Not to have lighted at the kirk
        But stopped in the kirkyard.

41   "For it 's oh and oh I prayed to God,
        Whose rest I hoped to win,
    That when to-night at your board-head
        You 'd bid the feast begin,
    This water past your window-sill
        Might bear my body in."

Stratton Water.

42

Now make the white bed warm and soft
And greet the merry morn.
The night the mother should have died,
The young son shall be born.

INTRODUCTION TO "THE STAFF AND SCRIP."

IN 1849 Rossetti writes to his brother that he has bought a translation, in two volumes, of the *Gesta Romanorum,* a book he had long wished to possess. He adds: "I was, however, rather disappointed, having expected to find lots of glorious stories for poems. Four or five good ones there are, one of which (which I have entitled *The Scrip and Staff*) I have considerably altered, and enclose for your opinion, together with another plot of my own devising. Both of these I contemplate versifying when free from existing nightmares."

The poem finally appeared in *The Oxford and Cambridge Magazine* under the title *The Staff and Scrip.* Canon Dixon says of it that, in his judgment, it is "the finest of all Rossetti's poems, and one of the most glorious writings in the language. It exhibits in flawless perfection the gift that he had above all other writers — absolute beauty and pure action."

THE STAFF AND SCRIP.[1]

"WHO rules these lands?" the Pilgrim said.
  "Stranger, Queen Blanchelys."
"And who has thus harried them?" he said.
  "It was Duke Luke did this:
      God's ban be his!"

The Pilgrim said: "Where is your house?
  I'll rest there, with your will."
"You've but to climb these blackened boughs
  And you'll see it over the hill,
      For it burns still."

"Which road, to seek your Queen?" said he.
  "Nay, nay, but with some wound
You'll fly back hither, it may be,
  And by your blood i' the ground
      My place be found."

"Friend, stay in peace.   God keep your head,
  And mine, where I will go;
For He is here and there," he said.
  He passed the hill-side, slow,
      And stood below.

The Queen sat idle by her loom:
  She heard the arras stir,
And looked up sadly: through the room
  The sweetness sickened her
      Of musk and myrrh.

The Staff and Scrip.

Her women, standing two and two,
  In silence combed the fleece.
The Pilgrim said, "Peace be with you,
  Lady"; and bent his knees.
      She answered, "Peace."

Her eyes were like the wave within;
  Like water-reeds the poise
Of her soft body, dainty thin;
  And like the water's noise
      Her plaintive voice.

For him, the stream had never well'd
  In desert tracks malign
So sweet; nor had he ever felt
  So faint in the sunshine
      Of Palestine.

Right so, he knew that he saw weep
  Each night through every dream[3]
The Queen's own face, confused in sleep
  With visages supreme
      Not known to him.

"Lady," he said, "your lands lie burnt
  And waste: to meet your foe
All fear: this I have seen and learnt.
  Say that it shall be so,
      And I will go."

She gazed at him.   "Your cause is just,
  For I have heard the same,"
He said: "God's strength shall be my trust.
  Fall it to good or grame,
      'T is in His name."

The Staff and Scrip.

"Sir, you are thanked. My cause is dead.
  Why should you toil to break
A grave, and fall therein?" she said.
  He did not pause but spake:
    "For my vow's sake."

"Can such vows be, Sir—to God's ear,
  Not to God's will?" "My vow
Remains: God heard me there as here,"
  He said with reverent brow, 4
    "Both then and now."

They gazed together, he and she,
  The minute while he spoke;
And when he ceased, she suddenly
  Looked round upon her folk
    As though she woke.

"Fight, Sir," she said; "my prayers in pain
  Shall be your fellowship."
He whispered one among her train,—
  "To-morrow bid her keep 5
    This staff and scrip."

She sent him a sharp sword, whose belt
  About his body there
As sweet as her own arms he felt.
  He kissed its blade, all bare,
    Instead of her.

She sent him a green banner wrought
  With one white lily stem,
To bind his lance with when he fought.
  He writ upon the same
    And kissed her name.

The Staff and Scrip.

She sent him a white shield, whereon
  She bade that he should trace
His will. He blent fair hues that shone,
  And in a golden space
    He kissed her face.

Born of the day that died, that eve [6]
  Now dying sank to rest;
As he, in likewise taking leave,
  Once with a heaving breast
    Looked to the west.

And there the sunset skies unseal'd, [7]
  Like lands he never knew,
Beyond to-morrow's battle-field
  Lay open out of view
    To ride into.

Next day till dark the women pray'd:
  Nor any might know there
How the fight went: the Queen has bade
  That there do come to her
    No messenger.

The Queen is pale, her maidens ail; [8]
  And to the organ-tones
They sing but faintly, who sang well
  The matin-orisons,
    The lauds and nones.

Lo, Father, is thine ear inclin'd,
  And hath thine angel passed?
For these thy watchers now are blind
  With vigil, and at last
    Dizzy with fast.

The Staff and Scrip.

Weak now to them the voice o' the priest
  As any trance affords;
And when each anthem failed and ceas'd,
  It seemed that the last chords
    Still sang the words.

"Oh what is the light that shines so red?
  'T is long since the sun set";
Quoth the youngest to the eldest maid;
  "'T was dim but now, and yet
    The light is great."

Quoth the other: "'T is our sight is dazed
  That we see flame i' the air."
But the Queen held her brows and gazed,
  And said, "It is the glare
    Of torches there."

"Oh what are the sounds that rise and spread?
  All day it was so still";
Quoth the youngest to the eldest maid:
  "Unto the furthest hill
    The air they fill."

Quoth the other: "'T is our sense is blurr'd
  With all the chants gone by."
But the Queen held her breath and heard,
  And said, "It is the cry
    Of Victory."

The first of all the rout was sound,
  The next were dust and flame,
And then the horses shook the ground:
  And in the thick of them
    A still band came.

The Staff and Scrip.

"Oh what do ye bring out of the fight,
  Thus hid beneath these boughs?"
"Thy conquering guest returns to-night,
  And yet shall not carouse,
    Queen, in thy house."

"Uncover ye his face," she said.
  "O changed in little space!"
She cried, "O pale that was so red!
  O God, O God of grace!
    Cover his face."

His sword was broken in his hand
  Where he had kissed the blade.
"O soft steel that could not withstand!
  O my hard heart unstayed,[10]
    That prayed and prayed!"

His bloodied banner crossed his mouth
  Where he had kissed her name.
"O east, and west, and north, and south,
  Fair flew my web, for shame,[11]
    To guide Death's aim!"

The tints were shredded from his shield
  Where he had kissed her face.
"Oh, of all gifts that I could yield,
  Death only keeps its place,
    My gift and grace!"

Then stepped a damsel to her side,
  And spoke, and needs must weep:
"For his sake, lady, if he died,
  He prayed of thee to keep
    This staff and scrip."

The Staff and Scrip.

That night they hung above her bed,
 Till morning wet with tears.
Year after year above her head
 Her bed his token wears,
  Five years, ten years.

That night the passion of her grief
 Shook them as there they hung.
Each year the wind that shed the leaf
 Shook them and in its tongue
  A message flung.

And once she woke with a clear mind[12]
 That letters writ to calm
Her soul lay in the scrip; to find[13]
 Only a torpid balm[14]
  And dust of palm.

They shook far off with palace sport
 When joust and dance were rife;
And the hunt shook them from the court;
 For hers, in peace or strife,
  Was a Queen's life.

A Queen's death now: as now they shake
 To gusts in chapel dim,—[15]
Hung where she sleeps, not seen to wake,
 (Carved lovely white and slim),
  With them by him.

Stand up to-day, still armed, with her,
 Good knight, before His brow
Who then as now was here and there,
 Who had in mind thy vow
  Then even as now.

The Staff and Scrip.

The lists are set in Heaven to-day,
  The bright pavilions shine;
Fair hangs thy shield, and none gainsay
  The trumpets sound in sign
    That she is thine.

Not tithed with days' and years' decease
  He pays thy wage He owed,
But with imperishable peace[16]
  Here in His own abode,
    Thy jealous God.

INTRODUCTION TO "SISTER HELEN."

WHAT Rossetti termed his "ghastly ballad" of *Sister Helen* was written in 1851 or 1852, and first printed in the English issue of a German magazine, named *The Düsseldorf Artists' Annual.* Rossetti signed it with the initials H. H. H., intending thereby to signify "the extreme hardness of his style," certain people having made that criticism—either from perversity or complete inanity.

The poem is based upon an old superstition to the effect that by burning the waxen image of any person whom you may wish to injure, that person is forced to die in torment.

Like most of Rossetti's essays in ballad form, *Sister Helen* is much too ornate and charged with hidden meanings to be classed with the old simple ballads of the people by which the word "ballad" has gained its direct meaning for us. But its emotional fervour and pictorial phraseology, together with the romantic spirit investing it, make it a wonderful performance of its own kind, which has neither prototype nor counterpart in our literature. It was revised for the volume of 1870, and fresh additions and revisions were made in 1880, much to the satisfaction of its author, who, at that period of his life, was taking his work with extreme—almost extravagant—seriousness. He wrote to Hall Caine:

"You will be horror-struck to hear that the first main addition to this poem was made by me only a few days

Introduction to "Sister Helen."

ago!—eight stanzas (six together, and two scattered ones) involving a new incident ! ! Your hair is on end, I know, but if you heard the stanzas, they would smooth if not curl it. The gain is immense." The six consecutive stanzas here referred to start from the line:

A lady's here, by a dark steed brought.

The two "scattered" stanzas inserted are the one beginning:

Three days ago on his marriage morn,

and the one beginning:

Flank to flank are the three steeds gone.

Three or four minor changes also were made in the phraseology.

SISTER HELEN.

(1853–80.)

"Why did you melt your waxen man,
     Sister Helen?
To-day is the third since you began."
"The time was long, yet the time ran,
     Little brother."
   (O Mother, Mary Mother,
Three days to-day, between Hell and Heaven!)

"But if you have done your work aright,
     Sister Helen,
You'll let me play, for you said I might."
"Be very still in your play to-night,
     Little brother."
   (O Mother, Mary Mother,
Third night, to-night, between Hell and Heaven!)

"You said it must melt ere vesper-bell,
     Sister Helen;
If now it be molten, all is well."
"Even so,—nay, peace! you cannot tell,
     Little brother."
   (O Mother, Mary Mother,
O what is this, between Hell and Heaven?)

Sister Helen.

4 "Oh, the waxen knave was plump to-day,
      Sister Helen;
How like dead folk he has dropped away!"
"Nay now, of the dead what can you say,
      Little brother?"
     (O Mother, Mary Mother,
What of the dead, between Hell and Heaven?)

5 "See, see, the sunken pile of wood,
      Sister Helen,
Shines through the thinned wax red as blood !"
"Nay now, when looked you yet on blood,
      Little brother?"
     (O Mother, Mary Mother,
How pale she is, between Hell and Heaven !)

6 "Now close your eyes, for they're sick and sore,
      Sister Helen,
And I'll play without the gallery door."
"Aye, let me rest,—I'll lie on the floor,
      Little brother."
     (O Mother, Mary Mother,
What rest to-night, between Hell and Heaven?)

 "Here high up in the balcony,
      Sister Helen,
The moon flies face to face with me."
"Aye, look and say whatever you see,
      Little brother."
     (O Mother, Mary Mother,
What sight to-night, between Hell and Heaven?)

Sister Helen.

Sister Helen.

Sister Helen.

12
"He has made a sign and called Halloo!
　　　　　　　Sister Helen,
And he says that he would speak with you."
"Oh tell him I fear the frozen dew,
　　　　　　　Little brother."
　　　　　(*O Mother, Mary Mother,*
Why laughs she thus, between Hell and Heaven?)

13
"The wind is loud, but I hear him cry,
　　　　　　　Sister Helen,
That Keith of Ewern's like to die."
"And he and thou, and thou and I,
　　　　　　　Little brother."
　　　　　(*O Mother, Mary Mother,*
And they and we, between Hell and Heaven!)

14
"Three days ago, on his marriage-morn,
　　　　　　　Sister Helen,
He sickened, and lies since then forlorn."
"For bridegroom's side is the bride a thorn,
　　　　　　　Little brother?"
　　　　　(*O Mother, Mary Mother,*
Cold bridal cheer, between Hell and Heaven!)

15
"Three days and nights he has lain abed,[1]
　　　　　　　Sister Helen,
And he prays in torment to be dead."
"The thing may chance, if he have prayed,
　　　　　　　Little brother!"
　　　　　(*O Mother, Mary Mother,*
If he have prayed, between Hell and Heaven!)

Sister Helen.

16

"But he has not ceased to cry to-day,
                  Sister Helen,
That you should take your curse away."
"*My* prayer was heard,—he need but pray,
                  Little brother!"
             (O Mother, Mary Mother,
Shall God not hear, between Hell and Heaven?)

17

"But he says, till you take back your ban,
                  Sister Helen,
His soul would pass, yet never can."
"Nay then, shall I slay a living man,
                  Little brother?"
             (O Mother, Mary Mother,
A living soul, between Hell and Heaven!)

18

"But he calls for ever on your name,
                  Sister Helen,
And says that he melts before a flame."
"My heart for his pleasure fared the same,
                  Little brother."
             (O Mother, Mary Mother,
Fire at the heart, between Hell and Heaven!)

19

"Here's Keith of Westholm riding fast,
                  Sister Helen,
For I know the white plume on the blast."
"The hour, the sweet hour I forecast,
                  Little brother!"
             (O Mother, Mary Mother,
Is the hour sweet, between Hell and Heaven?)

Sister Helen.

20   "He stops to speak, and he stills his horse,
                    Sister Helen;
But his words are drowned in the wind's course."
"Nay hear, nay hear, you must hear perforce,
                 Little brother!"
           (*O Mother, Mary Mother,*
What word now heard, between Hell and Heaven?)

21   "O he says that Keith of Ewern's cry,
                    Sister Helen,
Is ever to see you ere he die."
"In all that his soul sees, there am I,
                 Little brother!"
           (*O Mother, Mary Mother,*
The soul's one sight, between Hell and Heaven!)

22   "He sends a ring and a broken coin,
                    Sister Helen,
And bids you mind the banks of Boyne."
"What else he broke will he ever join,
                 Little brother?"
           (*O Mother, Mary Mother,*
No, never joined, between Hell and Heaven!)

23   "He yields you these and craves full fain,
                    Sister Helen,
You pardon him in his mortal pain."
"What else he took will he give again,
                 Little brother?"
           (*O Mother, Mary Mother,*
Not twice to give, between Hell and Heaven!)

Sister Helen.

24   "He calls your name in an agony,
                        Sister Helen,
That even dead Love must weep to see."
"Hate, born of Love, is blind as he,
                        Little brother!"
                        (O Mother, Mary Mother,
Love turned to hate, between Hell and Heaven!)

25   "Oh it's Keith of Keith now that rides fast,
                        Sister Helen,
For I know the white hair on the blast."
"The short, short hour will soon be past,
                        Little brother!"
                        (O Mother, Mary Mother,
Will soon be past, between Hell and Heaven!)

26   "He looks at me and he tries to speak,
                        Sister Helen,
But oh! his voice is sad and weak!"
"What here should the mighty Baron seek,
                        Little Brother?"
                        (O Mother, Mary Mother,
Is this the end, between Hell and Heaven?)

27   "Oh, his son still cries, if you forgive,
                        Sister Helen,
The body dies but the soul shall live."
"Fire shall forgive me as I forgive,
                        Little brother!"
                        (O Mother, Mary Mother,
As she forgives, between Hell and Heaven!)

Sister Helen.

28

"Oh he prays you, as his heart would rive,
               Sister Helen,
To save his dear son's soul alive."
"Fire cannot slay it, it shall thrive,
               Little brother!"
           (O Mother, Mary Mother,
Alas, alas, between Hell and Heaven!)

29

"He cries to you, kneeling in the road,
               Sister Helen,
To go with him for the love of God!"
"The way is long to his son's abode,
               Little brother."
           (O Mother, Mary Mother,
The way is long, between Hell and Heaven!)

30

"A lady 's here, by a dark steed brought,
               Sister Helen,
So darkly clad, I saw her not."
"See her now or never see aught,
               Little brother!"
           (O Mother, Mary Mother,
What more to see, between Hell and Heaven?)

31

"Her hood falls back, and the moon shines fair,
               Sister Helen,
On the Lady of Ewern's golden hair."
"Blest hour of my power and her despair,
               Little brother!"
           (O Mother, Mary Mother,
Hour blest and bann'd, between Hell and Heaven!)

Sister Helen.

32   "Pale, pale her cheeks, that in pride did glow,
       Sister Helen,
'Neath the bridal-wreath three days ago."
"One morn for pride and three days for woe,
       Little brother!"
     (*O Mother, Mary Mother,*
Three days, three nights, between Hell and Heaven!)

33   "Her clasped hands stretch from her bending head,
       Sister Helen;
With the loud wind's wail her sobs are wed."
"What wedding-strains hath her bridal-bed,
       Little brother?"
     (*O Mother, Mary Mother,*
What strain but death's between Hell and Heaven!)

34   "She may not speak, she sinks in a swoon,
       Sister Helen,—
She lifts her lips and gasps on the moon."
"Oh! might I but hear her soul's blithe tune,
       Little brother!"
     (*O Mother, Mary Mother,*
Her woe's dumb cry, between Hell and Heaven!)

35   "They 've caught her to Westholm's saddle-bow,
       Sister Helen,
And her moonlit hair gleams white in its flow."
"Let it turn whiter than winter snow,
       Little brother!"
     (*O Mother, Mary Mother,*
Woe-withered gold, between Hell and Heaven!)

Sister Helen.

"O sister Helen, you heard the bell.
          Sister Helen!
More loud than the vesper-chime it fell."
"No vesper-chime, but a dying knell,
          Little brother!"
          (O Mother, Mary Mother,
His dying knell, between Hell and Heaven!)

"Alas! but I fear the heavy sound,
          Sister Helen;
Is it in the sky or in the ground?"
"Say, have they turned their horses round,
          Little brother?"
          (O Mother, Mary Mother,
What would she more, between Hell and Heaven?)

"They have raised the old man from his knee,
          Sister Helen,
And they ride in silence hastily."
"More fast the naked soul doth flee,
          Little brother!"
          (O Mother, Mary Mother,
The naked soul, between Hell and Heaven!)

"Flank to flank are the three steeds gone,
          Sister Helen,
But the lady's dark steed goes alone."
"And lonely her bridegroom's soul hath flown,
          Little brother."
          (O Mother, Mary Mother,
The lonely ghost, between Hell and Heaven!)

Sister Helen.

"Oh, the wind is sad in the iron chill,
                    Sister Helen.
And weary and sad they look by the hill."
"But he and I are sadder still,
                    Little brother!"
          O Mother, Mary Mother,
Most sad of all, between Hell and Heaven!)

"See, see, the wax has dropped from its place,
                    Sister Helen,
And the flames are winning up apace!"
"Yet here they burn but for a space!
                    Little brother!"
          (O Mother, Mary Mother,
Here for a space, between Hell and Heaven!)

"Ah! what white thing at the door has cross'd,
                    Sister Helen?
Ah! what is this that sighs in the frost?"
"A soul that 's lost as mine is lost,
                    Little brother!"
          (O Mother, Mary Mother,
Lost, lost, all lost, between Hell and Heaven!)

ENGLISH MAY.[1]
(1854.)

WOULD God your health were as this month of May
   Should be, were this not England,—and your face
   Abroad, to give the gracious sunshine grace
And laugh beneath the budding hawthorn-spray.
But here the hedgerows pine from green to grey
   While yet May's lyre is tuning, and her song
   Is weak in shade that should in sun be strong;
And your pulse springs not to so faint a lay.

If in my life be breath of Italy,
   Would God that I might yield it all to you!
   So when such grafted warmth had burgeoned through
The languor of your Maytime's hawthorn-tree,
My spirit at rest should walk unseen and see
   The garland of your beauty bloom anew.

BEAUTY AND THE BIRD.

SHE fluted with her mouth as when one sips,
   And gently waved her golden head, inclin'd
   Outside his cage close to the window-blind;
Till her fond bird, with little turns and dips,
Piped low to her of sweet companionships.
   And when he made an end, some seed took she
   And fed him from her tongue, which rosily
Peeped as a piercing bud between her lips.

And like the child in Chaucer, on whose tongue
   The blessed Mary laid, when he was dead,
A grain,—who straightway praised her name in song:
   Even so, when she, a little lightly red,
Now turned on me and laughed, I heard the throng
   Of inner voices praise her golden head.

A NEW-YEAR'S BURDEN.

ALONG the grass sweet airs are blown
  Our way this day in Spring.
Of all the songs that we have known
  Now which one shall we sing?
        Not that, my love, ah no!—
        Not this, my love? why, so!—
Yet both were ours, but hours will come and go.

The grove is all a pale frail mist,
  The new year sucks the sun.
Of all the kisses that we kissed
  Now which shall be the one?
        Not that, my love, ah no!—
        Not this, my love?—heigh-ho
For all the sweets that all the winds can blow!

The branches cross above our eyes,
  The skies are in a net:
And what's the thing beneath the skies
  We two would most forget?
        Not birth, my love, no, no,—
        Not death, my love, no, no,—
The love once ours, but ours long hours ago.

Troy Town.

Sketc for Picture not executed 1870

PENUMBRA.

I DID not look upon her eyes,
(Though scarcely seen, with no surprise,
'Mid many eyes a single look,)
Because they should not gaze rebuke,
At night, from stars in sky and brook.

I did not take her by the hand,
(Though little was to understand
From touch of hand all friends might take,)
Because it should not prove a flake
Burnt in my palm to boil and ache.

I did not listen to her voice,
(Though none had noted, where at choice
All might rejoice in listening,)
Because no such a thing should cling
In the wood's moan at evening.

I did not cross her shadow once,
(Though from the hollow west the sun's
Last shadow runs along so far,)
Because in June it should not bar
My ways, at noon when fevers are.

They told me she was sad that day,
(Though wherefore tell what love's soothsay,
Sooner than they, did register?)
And my heart leapt and wept to her,
And yet I did not speak nor stir.

Penumbra.

So shall the tongues of the sea's foam
(Though many voices therewith come
From drowned hope's home to cry to me,)
Bewail one hour the more, when sea
And wind are one with memory.

A MATCH WITH THE MOON.

WEARY already, weary miles to-night
 I walked for bed: and so, to get some ease,
 I dogged the flying moon with similes.
And like a wisp she doubled on my sight
In ponds; and caught in tree-tops like a kite
 And in a globe of film all liquorish
 Swam full-faced like a silly silver fish;—
Last like a bubble shot the welkin's height
Where my road turned, and got behind me, and sent
 My wizened shadow craning round at me,
 And jeered, "So, step the measure,—one two three!"—
And if I faced on her, looked innocent.
But just at parting, halfway down a dell,
She kissed me for good-night. So you 'll not tell.

INTRODUCTION TO "LOVE'S NOCTURN."

ROSSETTI seems to have suffered many pangs of indecision in the revision of this poem for his 1870 volume. He writes to his brother that the first conception of the poem was of a man not yet in love who dreams vaguely of a woman who he thinks must exist for him. This is not so happy an idea, Rossetti decides, as to refer the love to a known and actual woman. One stanza stood in the way of the new interpretation and was cut out. The opening, which had been criticised as obscure, was changed, and Rossetti, noting the changes, continues: "I have also added three new stanzas towards the close of this poem, to develop the sudden flight of the bogie on finding another bogie by the girl's bed, which seemed funkyish, though of course the right thing if she was already in love." One very characteristic alteration deserves mention. "'Lamps of an *auspicious* soul,'" he writes, referring to the fourth line of the sixth stanza, "stood in my last correction (made long ago) 'pellucid,' which is much finer. But lately in the *Ring and Book* I came on *pellucid soul* applied to Caponsacchi, and the inevitable charge of plagiarism struck me at once as impending whenever my poem should be printed." In the present edition it will be seen that *translucent soul* solves the difficulty.

Mr. William Rossetti suggests that this poem was possibly the one sent in response to Mr. Norton's invita-

Love's Nocturn.

tion to Rossetti to contribute to the *Atlantic Monthly*, which in 1857 was just starting under Lowell's editorship. The poem that was sent was lost on the way, and though subsequently recovered was not printed, both Mr. Norton and Lowell finding it "foggy" reading, to use Rossetti's phrase.

LOVE'S NOCTURN.

MASTER of the murmuring courts
  Where the shapes of sleep convene! —
Lo! my spirit here exhorts
  All the powers of thy demesne
  For their aid to woo my queen.
          What reports
  Yield thy jealous courts unseen?

Vaporous, unaccountable.
  Dreamworld lies forlorn of light,
Hollow like a breathing shell.
  Ah! that from all dreams I might
  Choose one dream and guide its flight!
          I know well
  What her sleep should tell to-night.

There the dreams are multitudes:
  Some that will not wait for sleep,
Deep within the August woods;
  Some that hum while rest may steep
  Weary labour laid a-heap;
          Interludes,
  Some, of grievous moods that weep.

Poet's fancies all are there:
  There the elf-girls flood with wings
Valleys full of plaintive air;
  There breathe perfumes; there in rings

Love's Nocturn.

Whirl the foam-bewildered springs;
    Siren there
Winds her dizzy hair and sings.

Thence the one dream mutually
    Dreamed in bridal unison,
Less than waking ecstasy;
    Half-formed visions that make moan
    In the house of birth alone;
        And what we
At death's wicket see, unknown.

But for mine own sleep, it lies
    In one gracious form's control,
Fair with honourable eyes,
    Lamps of a translucent soul:
    O their glance is loftiest dole,
        Sweet and wise,
Wherein Love descries his goal.

Reft of her, my dreams are all
    Clammy trance that fears the sky:
Changing footpaths shift and fall;
    From polluted coverts nigh,
    Miserable phantoms sigh;
        Quakes the pall,
And the funeral goes by.

Master, is it soothly said
    That, as echoes of man's speech
Far in secret clefts are made,
    So do all men's bodies reach
    Shadows o'er thy sunken beach,—
        Shape or shade
In those halls pourtrayed of each?

Love's Nocturn.

Ah! might I, by thy good grace
  Groping in the windy stair,
(Darkness and the breath of space
  Like loud waters everywhere,)
  Meeting mine own image there
      Face to face,
  Send it from that place to her!

Nay, not I; but oh! do thou,
  Master, from thy shadowkind
Call my body's phantom now:
  Bid it bear its face declin'd
  Till its flight her slumbers find,
      And her brow
  Feel its presence bow like wind.

Where in groves the gracile Spring
  Trembles, with mute orison
Confidently strengthening,
  Water's voice and wind's as one
  Shed an echo in the sun.
      Soft as Spring,
  Master, bid it sing and moan.

Song shall tell how glad and strong
  Is the night she soothes alway;
Moan shall grieve with that parched tongue
  Of the brazen hours of day:
  Sounds as of the springtide they,
      Moan and song,
  While the chill months long for May.

Not the prayers which with all leave
  The world's fluent woes prefer,—

Love's Nocturn.

Not the praise the world doth give,
   Dulcet fulsome whisperer;—
Let it yield my love to her,
      And achieve
   Strength that shall not grieve or err.

Wheresoe'er my dreams befall,
   Both at night-watch, (let it say,)
And where round the sundial
   The reluctant hours of day,
   Heartless, hopeless of their way,
      Rest and call;—
   There her glance doth fall and stay.

Suddenly her face is there:
   So do mounting vapours wreathe
Subtle-scented transports where
   The black firwood sets its teeth.
   Part the boughs and look beneath,—
      Lilies share
   Secret waters there, and breathe.

Master, bid my shadow bend
   Whispering thus till birth of light,
Lest new shapes that sleep may send
   Scatter all its work to flight;—
   Master, master of the night,
      Bid it spend
   Speech, song, prayer, and end aright.

Yet, ah me! if at her head
   There another phantom lean
Murmuring o'er the fragrant bed,—
   Ah! and if my spirit's queen

Love's Nocturn.

Smile those alien prayers between,—[1]
　　Ah! poor shade!
Shall it strive, or fade unseen?

How should love's own messenger
　　Strive with love and be love's foe?
Master, nay! If thus, in her,
　　Sleep a wedded heart should show,—
　　Silent let mine image go,
　　　　Its old share
Of thy spell-bound air to know.[2]

Like a vapour wan and mute,
　　Like a flame, so let it pass;
One low sigh across her lute,
One dull breath against her glass;
　　And to my sad soul, alas!
　　　　One salute
Cold as when death's foot shall pass.

Then, too, let all hopes of mine,
　　All vain hopes by night and day,
Slowly at thy summoning sign
　　Rise up pallid and obey.
　　Dreams, if this is thus, were they:—
　　　　Be they thine,
And to dreamworld pine away.[3]

Yet from old time, life, not death,
　　Master, in thy rule is rife:
Lo! through thee, with mingling breath,
　　Adam woke beside his wife.
　　O Love bring me so, for strife,
　　　　Force and faith,
Bring me so not death but life!

Love's Nocturn.

Yea, to Love himself is pour'd
  This frail song of hope and fear.
Thou art Love, of one accord
  With kind Sleep to bring her near,
  Still-eyed, deep-eyed, ah how dear!
      Master, Lord,
  In her name implor'd, O hear!

ON CERTAIN ELIZABETHAN REVIVALS.

O RUFF-EMBASTIONED vast Elizabeth,
   Bush to these bushel-bellied casks of wine,
   Home-growth, 't is true, but rank as turpentine —
What would we with such skittle-plays at death?
Say, must we watch these brawlers' brandished lathe,
   Or to their reeking wit our ears incline,
   Because all Castaly flowed crystalline
In gentle Shakspeare's modulated breath?

What! must our drama with the rat-pit vie,
   Nor the scene close while one is left to kill?
     Shall this be poetry? And thou — thou man
     Of blood, thou cannibalic Caliban,
What shall be said of thee? A poet? — Fie!
   "An honourable murderer, if you will."

PLIGHTED PROMISE.

In a soft-complexioned sky,
  Fleeting rose and kindling grey,
Have you seen Aurora fly
  At the break of day?
So my maiden, so my plighted may
  Blushing cheek and gleaming eye
    Lifts to look my way.

Where the inmost leaf is stirred
  With the heart-beat of the grove,
Have you heard a hidden bird
  Cast her note above?
So my lady, so my lovely love,
  Echoing Cupid's prompted word,
    Makes a tune thereof.

Have you seen, at heaven's mid-height,
  In the moon-rack's ebb and tide,
Venus leap forth burning white,
  Dian pale and hide?
So my bright breast-jewel, so my bride,
  One sweet night, when fear takes flight,
    Shall leap against my side.

FIRST LOVE REMEMBERED.

Peace in her chamber, wheresoe'er
  It be, a holy place:
The thought still brings my soul such grace
  As morning meadows wear.

Whether it still be small and light,
  A maid's who dreams alone,
As from her orchard-gate the moon
  Its ceiling showed at night:

Or whether, in a shadow dense
  As nuptial hymns invoke,
Innocent maidenhood awoke
  To married innocence:

There still the thanks unheard await
  The unconscious gift bequeathed:
For there my soul this hour has breathed
  An air inviolate.

SUDDEN LIGHT.

I HAVE been here before,
  But when or how I cannot tell:
I know the grass beyond the door,
  The sweet, keen smell,
The sighing sound, the lights around the shore.

You have been mine before,—
  How long ago I may not know:
But just when at that swallow's soar
  Your neck turned so,
Some veil did fall,—I knew it all of yore.

Has this been thus before?[1]
  And shall not thus time's eddying flight
Still with our lives our love restore
  In death's despite,
And day and night yield one delight once more?

INTRODUCTION TO "EVEN SO."

COVENTRY PATMORE, commenting upon Rossetti's "extraordinary faculty for seeing objects in such a fierce light of imagination as very few poets have been able to throw upon external things," adds: "He can be forgiven for spoiling a tender lyric by a stanza such as this, which seems scratched with an adamantine pen upon a slab of agate:

> ' But the sea stands spread
> As one wall with the flat skies,
> Where the lean black craft, like flies,
> Seem well-nigh stagnated,
> Soon to drop off dead.' "

The stanza referred to is the poetic version of a prose passage in a letter from Rossetti to William Allingham, written in 1854. The passage — describing a June day at Hastings — runs as follows:

"There are dense fogs of heat here now, through which sea and sky loom as one wall, with the webbed craft creeping on it like flies, or standing there as if they would drop off dead. I wander over the baked cliffs, seeking rest and finding none."

EVEN SO.

So it is, my dear.
All such things touch secret strings
    For heavy hearts to hear.
    So it is, my dear.

    Very like indeed:
Sea and sky, afar, on high,
    Sand and strewn seaweed,—
    Very like indeed.

    But the sea stands spread
As one wall with the flat skies,
Where the lean black craft like flies
    Seem well-nigh stagnated,
    Soon to drop off dead.

    Seemed it so to us
When I was thine and thou wast mine,
    And all these things were thus,
    But all our world in us?

    Could we be so now?
Not if all beneath heaven's pall
    Lay dead but I and thou,
    Could we be so now!

THE WOODSPURGE.[1]

THE wind flapped loose, the wind was still,
Shaken out dead from tree and hill:
I had walked on at the wind's will,—
I sat now, for the wind was still.

Between my knees my forehead was,—
My lips, drawn in, said not Alas!
My hair was over in the grass,
My naked ears heard the day pass.

My eyes, wide open, had the run
Of some ten weeds to fix upon;
Among those few, out of the sun,
The woodspurge flowered, three cups in one.

From perfect grief there need not be
Wisdom or even memory:
One thing then learnt remains to me,—
The woodspurge has a cup of three.

THE HONEYSUCKLE.

I PLUCKED a honeysuckle where
   The hedge on high is quick with thorn,
   And climbing for the prize, was torn,
And fouled my feet in quag-water;
   And by the thorns and by the wind
   The blossom that I took was thinn'd,
And yet I found it sweet and fair.

Thence to a richer growth I came,
   Where, nursed in mellow intercourse,
   The honeysuckles sprang by scores,
Not harried like my single stem,
   All virgin lamps of scent and dew.
   So from my hand that first I threw,
Yet plucked not any more of them.

DANTIS TENEBRÆ.[1]

(In Memory of my Father.)

AND didst thou know indeed, when at the font
   Together with thy name thou gav'st me his,
   That also on thy son must Beatrice
Decline her eyes according to her wont,
Accepting me to be of those that haunt
   The vale of magical dark mysteries
   Where to the hills her poet's foot-track lies
And wisdom's living fountain to his chaunt
Trembles in music? This is that steep land
   Where he that holds his journey stands at gaze
     Tow'rd sunset, when the clouds like a new height
Seem piled to climb. These things I understand:
   For here, where day still soothes my lifted face,
     On thy bowed head, my father, fell the night.

WORDS ON THE WINDOW-PANE.[1]

Did she in summer write it, or in spring,
  Or with this wail of autumn at her ears,
  Or in some winter left among old years
Scratched it through tettered cark?   A certain thing
That round her heart the frost was hardening,
  Not to be thawed of tears, which on this pane
  Channelled the rime, perchance, in fevered rain,
For false man's sake and love's most bitter sting.

Howbeit, between this last word and the next
  Unwritten, subtly seasoned was the smart,
    And hère at least the grace to weep: if she,
Rather, midway in her disconsolate text,
  Rebelled not, loathing from the trodden heart
    That thing which she had found man's love to be.

THE SONG OF THE BOWER.

Say, is it day, is it dusk in thy bower,
　　Thou whom I long for, who longest for me?
Oh! be it light, be it night, 't is Love's hour,
　　Love's that is fettered as Love's that is free.
Free Love has leaped to that innermost chamber,
　　Oh! the last time, and the hundred before:
Fettered Love, motionless, can but remember,
　　Yet something that sighs from him passes the door.

Nay, but my heart when it flies to thy bower,
　　What does it find there that knows it again?
There it must droop like a shower-beaten flower,
　　Red at the rent core and dark with the rain.
Ah! yet what shelter is still shed above it, —
　　What waters still image its leaves torn apart?
Thy soul is the shade that clings round it to love it,
　　And tears are its mirror deep down in thy heart.

What were my prize, could I enter thy bower,
　　This day, to-morrow, at eve or at morn?
Large lovely arms and a neck like a tower,
　　Bosom then heaving that now lies forlorn.
Kindled with love-breath, (the sun's kiss is colder!)
　　Thy sweetness all near me, so distant to-day;
My hand round thy neck and thy hand on my shoulder
　　My mouth to thy mouth as the world melts away.

What is it keeps me afar from thy bower, —
　　My spirit, my body, so fain to be there?

The Song of the Bower.

Waters engulfing or fires that devour?—
  Earth heaped against me or death in the air?
Nay, but in day-dreams, for terror, for pity,
  The trees wave their heads with an omen to tell;
Nay, but in night-dreams, throughout the dark city,
  The hours, clashed together, lose count in the bell.

Shall I not one day remember thy bower,
  One day when all days are one day to me?—
Thinking, "I stirred not, and yet had the power!"—
  Yearning, "Ah God, if again it might be!"
Peace, peace! such a small lamp illumes, on this high-
    way,
  So dimly so few steps in front of my feet,—
Yet shows me that her way is parted from my way. . . .
  Out of sight, beyond light, at what goal may we
    meet?

DAWN ON THE NIGHT-JOURNEY.

TILL dawn the wind drove round me.   It is past
   And still, and leaves the air to lisp of bird,
   And to the quiet that is almost heard
Of the new-risen day, as yet bound fast
In the first warmth of sunrise.   When the last
   Of the sun's hours to-day shall be fulfilled,
   There shall another breath of time be stilled
For me, which now is to my senses cast
As much beyond me as eternity,
   Unknown, kept secret.   On the newborn air
The moth quivers in silence.   It is vast,
Yea, even beyond the hills upon the sea,
   The day whose end shall give this hour as sheer
As chaos to the irrevocable Past.

A LITTLE WHILE.

(1859.)

A LITTLE while a little love
 The hour yet bears for thee and me
 Who have not drawn the veil to see
If still our heaven be lit above.
Thou merely, at the day's last sigh,
 Hast felt thy soul prolong the tone;
And I have heard the night-wind cry
  And deemed its speech mine own.

A little while a little love
 The scattering autumn hoards for us
 Whose bower is not yet ruinous
Nor quite unleaved our songless grove.
Only across the shaken boughs
 We hear the flood-tides seek the sea,
And deep in both our hearts they rouse
  One wail for thee and me.

A little while a little love
 May yet be ours who have not said
 The word it makes our eyes afraid
To know that each is thinking of.
Not yet the end: be our lips dumb
 In smiles a little season yet:
I 'll tell thee, when the end is come,
  How we may best forget.

AN OLD SONG ENDED.

"How should I your true love know
  From another one?"
"By his cockle-hat and staff
  And his sandal-shoon."

"And what signs have told you now
  That he hastens home?"
"Lo! the spring is nearly gone,
  He is nearly come."

"For a token is there nought,
  Say, that he should bring?"
"He will bear a ring I gave
  And another ring."

"How may I, when he shall ask,
  Tell him who lies there?"
"Nay, but leave my face unveiled
  And unbound my hair."

"Can you say to me some word
  I shall say to him?"
"Say I'm looking in his eyes
  Though my eyes are dim."

INTRODUCTION TO " ASPECTA MEDUSA."

M R. WILLIAM ROSSETTI traces these verses to the year 1865. They were written for a design in pen and ink, from which Rossetti intended to paint a picture of Perseus allowing Andromeda to contemplate the severed head of Medusa as it was reflected from a tank of water. Rossetti's patrons could not, however, bring their minds to purchase so " horrid " a picture, and he left the subject unpainted.

The word "hankered " in the second line of the poem is certainly not a common one in poetry, but the Rossettis seem to have fancied it, as Christina also uses it in one of her loveliest poems, speaking of

> The foolishest fond folly of a heart
> That hankers after Heaven but clings to earth.

ASPECTA MEDUSA.

(For a Drawing.)

(1865.)

Andromeda, by Perseus saved and wed,
Hankered each day to see the Gorgon's head:
Till o'er a fount he held it, bade her lean,
And mirrored in the wave was safely seen
That death she lived by.

        Let not thine eyes know
Any forbidden thing itself, although
It once should save as well as kill: but be
Its shadow upon life enough for thee.

MICHAEL SCOTT'S WOOING.[1]

(For a Drawing.)

ROSE-SHEATHED beside the rosebud tongue
  Lurks the young adder's-tooth;
  Milk-mild from new-born hemlock-bluth
The earliest drops are wrung:
  And sweet the flower of his first youth
When Michael Scott was young.

INTRODUCTION TO "VENUS VERTI-CORDIA."

THE picture inspiring these verses stands quite by itself among Rossetti's paintings. For one thing, it is a departure from his usual habit of painting only draped figures. He painted two pictures of the subject, one a water-colour, one an oil, and writes thus concerning them: "I really do not think the large picture chargeable with anything like Ettyism, which I detest; but I am sure the little one has not a shadow of it. Drapery of any kind I could not introduce without quite killing my own idea." Over the flowers in the picture he worked with true pre-Raphaelite patience. He writes to his mother:

"I am tied down to my canvas till all the flower part of it is finished. I have done many more roses, and have established an arrangement with a nursery-gardener at Cheshunt whereby they reach me every two days at 2s. 6d. for a couple of dozen each time, which is better than paying a shilling apiece at Covent Garden. Also honeysuckles I have succeeded in getting at the Crystal Palace, and have painted a lot already in my foreground, and hope for more." All this took a week of searching; Rossetti can hardly have been cheered by Ruskin's comment on the result. The flowers he deemed " wonderful" in their realism, and "awful" in their "coarseness."

VENUS VERTICORDIA.

(For a Picture.)

SHE hath the apple in her hand for thee,
   Yet almost in her heart would hold it back;
   She muses, with her eyes upon the track
Of that which in thy spirit they can see.
Haply, "Behold, he is at peace," saith she;
   "Alas! the apple for his lips,—the dart
   That follows its brief sweetness to his heart,—
The wandering of his feet perpetually!"

A little space her glance is still and coy;
   But if she give the fruit that works her spell,
Those eyes shall flame as for her Phrygian boy.
   Then shall her bird's strained throat the woe foretell,
   And her far seas moan as a single shell,
And through her dark grove strike the light of Troy.[1]

EDEN BOWER.[1]

IT was Lilith the wife of Adam:
                (Sing Eden Bower!)[2]
Not a drop of her blood was human,
But she was made like a soft sweet woman.

Lilith stood on the skirts of Eden;
                (Alas the hour!)
She was the first that thence was driven;
With her was hell and with Eve was heaven.

In the ear of the Snake said Lilith:—
                (Sing Eden Bower!)
"To thee I come when the rest is over;
A snake was I when thou wast my lover.

"I was the fairest snake in Eden;
                (Alas the hour!)
By the earth's will, new form and feature
Made me a wife for the earth's new creature.

"Take me thou as I come from Adam:
                (Sing Eden Bower!)
Once again shall my love subdue thee;
The past is past and I am come to thee.

"O but Adam was thrall to Lilith!
                (Alas the hour!)
All the threads of my hair are golden,
And there in a net his heart was holden.

Eden Bower.

"O and Lilith was queen of Adam!
                    (*Sing Eden Bower!*)
All the day and night together
My breath could shake his soul like a feather.

"What great joys had Adam and Lilith!—
                    (*Alas the hour!*)
Sweet close rings of the serpent's twining,
As heart in heart lay sighing and pining.

"What bright babes had Lilith and Adam!—
                    (*Sing Eden Bower!*)
Shapes that coiled in the woods and waters,
Glittering sons and radiant daughters.

"O thou God, the Lord God of Eden!
                    (*Alas the hour!*)
Say, was this fair body for no man,
That of Adam's flesh thou mak'st him a woman?

"O thou Snake, the King-snake of Eden!
                    (*Sing Eden Bower!*)
God's strong will our necks are under,
But thou and I may cleave it in sunder.

"Help, sweet Snake, sweet lover of Lilith!
                    (*Alas the hour!*)
And let God learn how I loved and hated
Man in the image of God created.

"Help me once against Eve and Adam!
                    (*Sing Eden Bower!*)
Help me once for this one endeavour,
And then my love shall be thine for ever!

Eden Bower.

"Strong is God, the fell foe of Lilith:
          (Alas the hour!)
Nought in heaven or earth may affright Him;
But join thou with me and we will smite Him.

"Strong is God, the great God of Eden:
          (Sing Eden Bower!)
Over all He made He hath power;
But lend me thou thy shape for an hour!

"Lend thy shape for the love of Lilith!
          (Alas the hour!)
Look, my mouth and my cheek are ruddy,
And thou art cold, and fire is my body.

"Lend thy shape for the hate of Adam!
          (Sing Eden Bower!)
That he may wail my joy that forsook him,
And curse the day when the bride-sleep took him.

"Lend thy shape for the shame of Eden!
          (Alas the hour!)
Is not the foe-God weak as the foeman
When love grows hate in the heart of a woman?

"Wouldst thou know the heart's hope of Lilith?
          (Sing Eden Bower!)
Then bring thou close thine head till it glisten
Along my breast, and lip me and listen.

"Am I sweet, O sweet Snake of Eden?
          (Alas the hour!)
Then ope thine ear to my warm mouth's cooing
And learn what deed remains for our doing.

Eden Bower.

"Thou didst hear when God said to Adam:—
          (*Sing Eden Bower!*)
'Of all this wealth I have made thee warden;
Thou 'rt free to eat of the trees of the garden:

" 'Only of one tree eat not in Eden;
          (*Alas the hour!*)
All save one I give to thy freewill,—
The Tree of the Knowledge of Good and Evil.'

"O my love, come nearer to Lilith!
          (*Sing Eden Bower!*)
In thy sweet folds bind me and bend me,
And let me feel the shape thou shalt lend me.

"In thy shape I 'll go back to Eden;
          (*Alas the hour!*)
In these coils that Tree will I grapple,
And stretch this crowned head forth by the apple.

"Lo, Eve bends to the breath of Lilith!
          (*Sing Eden Bower!*)
O how then shall my heart desire
All her blood as food to its fire!

"Lo, Eve bends to the words of Lilith!—
          (*Alas the hour!*)
'Nay, this Tree's fruit,—why should ye hate it,
Or Death be born the day that ye ate it?

" 'Nay, but on that great day in Eden,
          (*Sing Eden Bower!*)
By the help that in this wise Tree is,
God knows well ye shall be as He is.'

Eden Bower.

"Then Eve shall eat and give unto Adam;
        (*Alas the hour!*)
And then they both shall know they are naked,
And their hearts ache as my heart hath achèd.

"Ay, let them hide 'mid the trees of Eden,
        (*Sing Eden Bower!*)
As in the cool of the day in the garden
God shall walk without pity or pardon.

"Hear, thou Eve, the man's heart in Adam!
        (*Alas the hour!*)
Of his brave words hark to the bravest:—
'This the woman gave that thou gavest.'

"Hear Eve speak, yea list to her, Lilith!
        (*Sing Eden Bower!*)
Feast thine heart with words that shall sate it—
'This the serpent gave and I ate it.'

"O proud Eve, cling close to thine Adam,
        (*Alas the hour!*)
Driven forth as the beasts of his naming
By the sword that for ever is flaming.

"Know, thy path is known unto Lilith!
        (*Sing Eden Bower!*)
While the blithe birds sang at thy wedding,
There her tears grew thorns for thy treading.

"O my love, thou Love-snake of Eden!
        (*Alas the hour!*)
O to-day and the day to come after!
Loose me, love,—give breath to my laughter.

Eden Bower.

"O bright Snake, the Death-worm of Adam!
       (Sing Eden Bower!)
Wreathe thy neck with my hair's bright tether,
And wear my gold and thy gold together!

"On that day on the skirts of Eden,
       (Alas the hour!)
In thy shape shall I glide back to thee,
And in my shape for an instant view thee.

"But when thou 'rt thou and Lilith is Lilith,
       (Sing Eden Bower!)
In what bliss past hearing or seeing
Shall each one drink of the other's being!

"With cries of 'Eve!' and 'Eden!' and 'Adam!'
       (Alas the hour!)
How shall we mingle our love's caresses,
I in thy coils, and thou in my tresses!

"With those names, ye echoes of Eden,
       (Sing Eden Bower!)
Fire shall cry from my heart that burneth,—
'Dust he is and to dust returneth!'

"Yet to-day, thou master of Lilith,—
       (Alas the hour!)
Wrap me round in the form I 'll borrow
And let me tell thee of sweet to-morrow.

"In the planted garden eastward in Eden,
       (Sing Eden Bower!)
Where the river goes forth to water the garden,
The springs shall dry and the soil shall harden.

Eden Bower.

"Yea, where the bride-sleep fell upon Adam,
            (*Alas the hour!*)
None shall hear when the storm-wind whistles
Through roses choked among thorns and thistles.

"Yea, beside the east-gate of Eden,
            (*Sing Eden Bower!*)
Where God joined them and none might sever,
The sword turns this way and that for ever.

"What of Adam cast out of Eden?
            (*Alas the hour!*)
Lo! with care like a shadow shaken,
He tills the hard earth whence he was taken.

"What of Eve too, cast out of Eden?
            (*Sing Eden Bower!*)
Nay, but she, the bride of God's giving,
Must yet be mother of all men living.

"Lo, God's grace, by the grace of Lilith!
            (*Alas the hour!*)
To Eve's womb, from our sweet to-morrow,
God shall greatly multiply sorrow.

"Fold me fast, O God-snake of Eden!
            (*Sing Eden Bower!*)
What more prize than love to impel thee?
Grip and lip my limbs as I tell thee!

"Lo! two babes for Eve and for Adam!
            (*Alas the hour!*)
Lo! sweet Snake, the travail and treasure,—
Two men-children born for their pleasure!

Eden Bower.

" The first is Cain and the second Abel:
    (Sing Eden Bower!)
The soul of one shall be made thy brother,
And thy tongue shall lap the blood of the other."
    (Alas the hour!)

INTRODUCTION TO "MARY MAGDA-
LENE AT THE DOOR OF SIMON
THE PHARISEE."

THESE verses are ascribed by Mr. William Rossetti to
the year 1859; but I think they were written in
1869, judging from Rossetti's references to them, and
with very imperfect logic I have decided in this instance
to follow my own impression and place them among the
writings of that year, although in other similar instances
I have followed the order prescribed by Mr. William
Rossetti's list. The subject was in Rossetti's mind as
suitable for a picture as early as 1853, and he made many
drawings of it. The following is his description in
prose, written for the oil-painting of 1865:

"The scene represents two houses opposite each
other, one of which is that of Simon the Pharisee, where
Christ and Simon, with other guests, are seated at table.
In the opposite house a great banquet is held, and feast-
ers are trooping to it dressed in cloth of gold and crowned
with flowers. The musicians play at the door, and each
couple kiss as they enter. Mary Magdalene has been in
this procession, but has suddenly turned aside at the
sight of Christ, and is pressing forward up the steps of
Simon's house, and casting the roses from her hair.
Her lover and a woman have followed her out of the
procession and are laughingly trying to turn her back.
The woman bars the door with her arm. Those nearest
the Magdalene in the group of feasters have stopped

short in wonder and are looking after her, while a beggar-girl offers them flowers from her basket.   A girl near the front of the procession has caught sight of Mary and waves her garland to turn her back.   Beyond this, the narrow street abuts on the highroad and river.   The young girl seated on the steps is a little beggar who has had food given her from within the house, and is wondering to see Mary go in there, knowing her as a famous woman in the city.   Simon looks disdainfully at her, and the servant who is setting a dish on the table smiles, knowing her too.   Christ looks toward her from within, waiting till she shall reach him."

The head of Christ was drawn from Sir Edward Burne-Jones.

In 1869 Rossetti writes to his brother that he is then sending to the printer seven new sonnets, among them "one for Magdalene."

MARY MAGDALENE.[1]

AT THE DOOR OF SIMON THE PHARISEE.

(For a Drawing.[1])

" WHY wilt thou cast the roses from thine hair?
  Nay, be thou all a rose,—wreath, lips, and cheek.
  Nay, not this house,—that banquet-house we seek;
See how they kiss and enter; come thou there.
This delicate day of love we two will share
  Till at our ear love's whispering night shall speak.
  What, sweet one,—hold'st thou still the foolish freak?
Nay, when I kiss thy feet they 'll leave the stair."

" Oh loose me! Seest thou not my Bridegroom's face
  That draws me to Him? For His feet my kiss,
    My hair, my tears He craves to-day:—and oh!
What words can tell what other day and place
  Shall see me clasp those blood-stained feet of His?
    He needs me, calls me, loves me: let me go!"

TROY TOWN.[1]

Heavenborn Helen, Sparta's queen,
      (O Troy Town!)
Had two breasts of heavenly sheen,
The sun and moon of the heart's desire:
All Love's lordship lay between.
      (O Troy 's down,
      Tall Troy 's on fire!)

Helen knelt at Venus' shrine,
      (O Troy Town!)
Saying, " A little gift is mine,
A little gift for a heart's desire.
Hear me speak and make me a sign!
      (O Troy 's down,
      Tall Troy 's on fire!)

"Look, I bring thee a carven cup;
      (O Troy Town!)
See it here as I hold it up,—
Shaped it is to the heart's desire,
Fit to fill when the gods would sup.
      (O Troy 's down,
      Tall Troy 's on fire!)

"It was moulded like my breast;
      (O Troy Town!)
He that sees it may not rest,
Rest at all for his heart's desire.

Troy Town.

O give ear to my heart's behest!
       (O Troy 's down,
       Tall Troy 's on fire!)

"See my breast, how like it is;
       (O Troy Town!)
See it bare for the air to kiss!
Is the cup to thy heart's desire?
O for the breast, O make it his!
       (O Troy 's down,
       Tall Troy 's on fire!)

"Yea, for my bosom here I sue;
       (O Troy Town!)
Thou must give it where 't is due,
Give it there to the heart's desire.
Whom do I give my bosom to?
       (O Troy 's down,
       Tall Troy 's on fire!)

" Each twin breast is an apple sweet.
       (O Troy Town!)
Once an apple stirred the beat
Of thy heart with the heart's desire:—
Say, who brought it then to thy feet?
       (O Troy 's down,
       Tall Troy 's on fire!)

" They that claimed it then were three:
       (O Troy Town!)
For thy sake two hearts did he
Make forlorn of the heart's desire.
Do for him as he did for thee!
       (O Troy 's down,
       Tall Troy 's on fire!)

Troy Town.

"Mine are apples grown to the south,
    (*O Troy Town!*)
Grown to taste in the days of drouth,
Taste and waste to the heart's desire:
Mine are apples meet for his mouth."
    (*O Troy 's down,*
    Tall Troy 's on fire!)

Venus looked on Helen's gift,
    (*O Troy Town!*)
Looked and smiled with subtle drift,
Saw the work of her heart's desire:—
"There thou kneel'st for Love to lift!"
    (*O Troy 's down,*
    Tall Troy 's on fire!)

Venus looked in Helen's face,
    (*O Troy Town!*)
Knew far off an hour and place,
And fire lit from the heart's desire;
Laughed and said, "Thy gift hath grace!"
    (*O Troy 's down,*
    Tall Troy 's on fire!)

Cupid looked on Helen's breast,
    (*O Troy Town!*)
Saw the heart within its nest,
Saw the flame of the heart's desire,—
Marked his arrow's burning crest.
    (*O Troy 's down,*
    Tall Troy 's on fire!)

Cupid took another dart,
    (*O Troy Town!*)
Fledged it for another heart,

Troy Town.

Winged the shaft with the heart's desire,
Drew the string and said, "Depart!"
>   (*O Troy 's down,*
>   *Tall Troy 's on fire!*)

Paris turned upon his bed,
>   (*O Troy Town!*)
Turned upon his bed and said,
Dead at heart with the heart's desire —
"Oh to clasp her golden head I"
>   (*O Troy 's down,*
>   *Tall Troy 's on fire!*)

NOTES.

NOTES.

The Blessed Damozel. As printed in *The Oxford and Cambridge Magazine*, 1856. (Page 41.)

(1) Her eyes knew more of rest and shade
    Than waters still'd at even;
(2) And her hair lying down her back
(3) She scarcely heard her sweet new friends :
    Playing at holy games,
    Softly they spake among themselves
    Their virginal chaste names;
(In the 1870 version these lines are as follows:
    Heard hardly, some of her new friends
    Amid their loving games
    Spake evermore among themselves
    Their virginal chaste names;)
(4) And still she bow'd above the vast
    Waste sea of worlds that swarm;
(5) Had when they sung together,
(6) In the later versions this stanza is the eleventh. In the Oxford
    and Cambridge version it is the sixteenth.
(7) And we will step down as to a stream,
(8) This stanza is omitted in the Oxford and Cambridge version.
(9) The unnumber'd ransom'd heads
(10) At peace — only to be
(11) The light thrilled past her, fill'd
(12) And then she laid her arms along
In the 1870 version : "And then she cast her arms along."

My Sister's Sleep. (Page 50.)

(1) This poem is remarkable as an instance of sympathetic imagination,
    no death having occurred in Rossetti's family when it was written.

Jenny. (Page 59.)

(1) "*Mirth* and woe " in the 1870 edition.
(2) "With Raffael's or Da Vinci's hand " (1870).
(3) This line and the two following it do not appear in the 1870
    volume.

Notes.

At the Sunrise in 1848. (Page 74.)

(1) Referring to the European revolutions of this year.

Autumn Song (1848.) (Page 75.)

(1) This lyric was set to music by Mr. Dannreuther in 1877.

A Trip to Paris and Belgium. (Page 89.)

I. London to Folkestone.

(1) The last lines in Rossetti's first draught read:
I was roused altogether and looked out
To where, upon the desolate verge of light,
Yearned, pale and vast, the iron-coloured sea.

For a Virgin and Child. (Page 100.)

(1) In *The Germ* version this line reads:
While like a heavy flood the darkness ran.

For Ruggiero and Angelica. (Page 108.)

(1) The title in *The Germ* reads: " Angelica Rescued from the Sea-Monster," by Ingres; in the Luxembourg. The octave is not separated from the sestet.

Ave. (Page 113.)

(1) A church legend of the Blessed Virgin's death.
In the 1870 edition this line reads:
That day when death was sent to break.
(2) In the 1870 edition:
The cherubim, arrayed, conjoint.

Dante at Verona. (Page 127.)

(1) *Donne che avete intelletto d'amore:*—the first canzone of the *Vita Nuova*. (Rossetti's note.)
(2) Uguccione della Faggiuola, Dante's former protector, was now his fellow-guest at Verona. (Rossetti's note).
(3) " *Messere, voi non vedreste tant 'ossa se cane io fossi.*" The point of the reproach is difficult to render, depending as it does on the literal meaning of the name *Cane*. (Rossetti's note.)
(4) Such was the last sentence passed by Florence against Dante, as a recalcitrant exile.
(5) *E quindi uscimmo a riveder le stelle.*— INFERNO.
Puro e disposto a salire alle stelle.— PURGATORIO.
L'amor che muove il sole e l' altre stelle.—PARADISO. (Rossetti's note).
(6) *Quomodo sedet sola civitas!* — The words quoted by Dante in the *Vita Nuova* when he speaks of the death of Beatrice.

Notes.

A Last Confession.   (Page 147.)

(1) " Were red " (1870 edition).

(2) In the 1870 edition these lines read:
> —— till it seemed
> Within the whirling brain's entanglement
> That she or I or all things bled to death.
> And then I found her lying at my feet
> And knew that I had stabbed her, and saw still
> The look she gave me when she took the knife
> Deep in her heart; —

(3) " blade " (1870).

The Burden of Nineveh.   (Page 175.)

(1) During the excavations, the Tiyari workmen held their services in the shadow of the great bulls. — (Layard's *Nineveh*, ch. ix.)

The Church-Porch.   (Page 182.)

(1) A second sonnet on this subject was written by Rossetti but never published by him.   It appeared in the *Century Magazine* in 1882.

Wellington's Funeral.   (Page 183.)

(1) Date of the *Coup d'État*, 2d December, 1851.

The Staff and Scrip.   (Page 195.)

(1) In the Oxford and Cambridge version the following quotation is printed under the title:
> " How should I your true love know from another one ? "
> " By his cockle-hat and staff and his sandal-shoon."

(2) " owns " replaces " rules " in Oxford and Cambridge version.

(3) " throughout some dream " (Oxford and Cambridge).

(4) " bow " (Oxford and Cambridge).

(5) " To-night thou 'lt bid her keep " (Oxford and Cambridge).

(6) In the Oxford and Cambridge version this stanza reads:
> So arming through his soul there pass'd
>   Thoughts of all depth and height:
> But more than other things at last
>   Seem'd to the arm'd knight
>   The joy to fight.

(7) The skies by sunset all unseal'd
>   Long lands he never knew (Oxford and Cambridge).

(8) This and the next stanza are omitted in the Oxford and Cambridge version.

(9) " But the Queen held her brows —" (Oxford and Cambridge).

(10) " O harder heart unstayed " (Oxford and Cambridge).

(11) " Fair flew these folds —" (Oxford and Cambridge).

(12) " And she would wake —" (Oxford and Cambridge).

(13) " —— and find " (Oxford and Cambridge).

Notes.

(14) " Pink shells, a torpid balm " (Oxford and Cambridge).
(15) " To chaunts in chapel dim " (Oxford and Cambridge).
(16) " But in light stalls of golden peace " (Oxford and Cambridge).

Sister Helen. (Page 205.)

(1) But Keith of Ewern 's sadder still (1870).
(2) He sees me in earth, in moon and sky (1870).
(3) Earth, moon and sky, between Hell and Heaven (1870).
(4) Oh, never more, between Hell and Heaven (1870).
(5) No more again, between Hell and Heaven! (1870.)
(6) " For three days now " etc.— (1870).

English May. (Page 216.)

(1) This sonnet was probably addressed to Elizabeth Siddal, to whom
Rossetti was engaged, and whose health was a constant cause
of anxiety.

The Passover in the Holy Family. (Page 218.)

(1) Mr. William Rossetti attributes this sonnet to the year 1855, and
his chronological order is followed in giving it the place it has in
the present sequence of poems. From Rossetti's correspondence it
would appear, however, that it was one of seven sonnets written
in 1869.
(2) The scene is in the house-porch, where Christ holds a bowl of
blood from which Zacharias is sprinkling the posts and lintel. Jo-
seph has brought the lamb and Elizabeth lights the pyre. The
shoes which John fastens and the bitter herbs which Mary is gather-
ing form part of the ritual.

On the Site of a Mulberry-Tree. (Page 219.)

(1) The last line of this sonnet read originally:
Some tailor's ninth allotment of a ghost.
This Rossetti considered insulting to the worshipful body of tailors
and would not publish the sonnet lest it offend them. Finally in
MS. he substituted " starveling's " for " tailor's."

Love's Nocturn. (Page 226.)

(1) " Smile those alien words between " (1870).
(2) In the 1870 volume the word " sunken " replaced " spell-bound."
(3) " Dreamland " in the 1870 volume.

Sudden Light. (Page 235.)

(1) Then, now,— perchance again !
    O round mine eyes your tresses shake!
Shall we not lie as we have lain
    Thus for Love's sake,
    And sleep, and wake, yet never break the chain ? (1870.)

Notes.

The Woodspurge. (Page 238.)

(1) The "nature lore" in *The Woodspurge* is somewhat misleading. It was written by Rossetti in pursuance of a self-imposed stint, he having at one time resolved to turn out a poem a day. Coming in one afternoon in a mood of idleness he sat racking his brain for an idea, and turning over the leaves of a book on plants. A drawing of the woodspurge attracted his attention, and this poem was the result.

Dantis Tenebræ. (Page 240.)

(1) Dante Gabriel Rossetti was named for his father and for Dante Alighieri, of whose works Gabriele Rossetti was a passionate student.

Words on the Window-Pane. (Page 241.)

(1) For a woman's fragmentary inscription.

Michael Scott's Wooing. (Page 249.)

(1) The subject of *Michael Scott's Wooing* was frequently in Rossetti's mind. As early as 1848 he made a pen-and-ink design for it, and one in crayon — a different composition — in 1866. A number of years later he did a water-colour. The verse was probably written for the crayon drawing.

Venus Verticordia. (Page 251.)

(1) In the 1870 volume this last line reads:
And her grove glow with love-lit fires of Troy.

Eden Bower. (Page 252.)

(1) The Rabbinical legends of Lilith, the first wife of Adam, provided the suggestion for this thoroughly disagreeable poem. Mr. Knight comments upon it:
"The period during which a subject such as this had attraction for Rossetti was not long, and it is fortunate for his fame that it was not." It was the period during which insomnia began to rule his nights, and the breaking down of his health came well in view.
(2) In the 1870 volume the refrain ran in place of "Sing Eden Bower" "Eden bower 's in flower," and in place of " Alas the hour!" "And O the bower and the hour!"

Mary Magdalene. (Page 262.)

(1) In the drawing Mary has left a procession of revellers, and is ascending by a sudden impulse the steps of the house where she sees Christ. Her lover has followed her, and is trying to turn her back.

Troy Town. (Page 263.)

(1) The subject of this poem is Helen's dedication to Aphrodite of the goblet modelled in the shape of her breast. The legend is found in Pliny. ·

END OF VOL. I.

Lightning Source UK Ltd.
Milton Keynes UK
UKHW02f2151130918
328856UK00019B/497/P